MALTESE

JENNY DRASTURA

Maltese

Editor: Matthew Haviland
Indexer: Elizabeth Walker
Designer: Angela Stanford
Series Designer: Mary Ann Kahn

TFH Publications
President/CEO: Glen S. Axelrod
Executive Vice President: Mark E. Johnson
Publisher: Albert Connelly, Jr.
Associate Publisher: Stephanie Fornino

TFH Publications, Inc.
One TFH Plaza
Third and Union Avenues
Neptune City, NJ 07753

Marjorie Kaplan,President and General Manager, Animal Planet Media/Nicolas Bonard, GM & SVP, Discovery Studios Group/Robert Marick, VP, North American Licensing/Sue Perez-Jackson, Director, Licensing/Tracy Conner, Manager, Licensing

Printed and bound in China

15 16 17 18 19 20 1 3 5 7 9 8 6 4 2

Library of Congress Cataloging-in-Publication Data
Drastura, Jenny.
  Maltese / Jenny Drastura.
     pages cm. -- (Animal planet. Dogs 101)
  Includes bibliographical references and index.
  ISBN 978-0-7938-3735-9 (hardcover : alk. paper) 1. Maltese dog. I. Title.
  SF429.M25D73 2015
  636.76--dc23
                      2014039261

This book has been published with the intent to provide accurate and authoritative information in regard to the subject matter within. While every reasonable precaution has been taken in preparation of this book, the author and publisher expressly disclaim responsibility for any errors, omissions, or adverse effects arising from the use or application of the information contained herein. The techniques and suggestions are used at the reader's discretion and are not to be considered a substitute for veterinary care. If you suspect a medical problem consult your veterinarian.

Note: In the interest of concise writing, "he" is used when referring to puppies and dogs unless the text is specifically referring to females or males. "She" is used when referring to people. However, the information contained herein is equally applicable to both sexes.

The Leader In Responsible Animal Care for Over 50 Years!®
www.tfh.com

CENTRAL
Garden & Pet

CONTENTS

1 ORIGINS OF YOUR MALTESE 4

2 CHARACTERISTICS OF YOUR MALTESE 14

3 SUPPLIES FOR YOUR MALTESE 28

4 FEEDING YOUR MALTESE 40

5 GROOMING YOUR MALTESE 54

6 HEALTH OF YOUR MALTESE 70

7 TRAINING YOUR MALTESE 92

8 SOLVING PROBLEMS WITH YOUR MALTESE 108

9 ACTIVITIES WITH YOUR MALTESE 120

RESOURCES 132

INDEX 137

ORIGINS OF YOUR MALTESE

Maltese are clearly not just another pretty face!

One breed that stands out physically among all others in the world of dogs is the Maltese, Ye Ancient Dogge of Malta. Perhaps it's the diminutive size—4 to 6 pounds (2 to 2.5 kg) is about right. It could be the intense, round black eyes that entice you to give them a treat or toss their favorite toy. However, it is most likely the startlingly white flowing coat that surrounds the little dogs like a fluffy cloud when they pounce to the ground in play.

Maltese are delightful to watch as they glide across the floor at a breed competition and a joy to hold on your lap for love and comfort. They are just as precious to watch sporting a short puppy cut, chasing a ball across the floor. Maltese are showing up more and more at competitions such as obedience, rally, agility—even tracking, right along with the hound breeds! With this degree of intelligence and athletic ability, they are clearly not just another pretty face.

DEVELOPMENT OF THE DOG

A 33,000-year-old dog skull discovered in the Siberian Altai Mountains and dog remains found in a Belgian cave suggest the domestication of dogs occurred throughout early human history at different geographic locations. These findings could mean modern dogs have multiple ancestors rather than a single common ancestor, as DNA evidence had previously indicated.

Fossil records in Europe show that humans domesticated dogs about 18,000 years ago, possibly from a population of gray wolves now extinct. The generally accepted scenario is that a pack of wolves would observe humans discarding food at the outskirts of a camp and eat there rather than going hunting. As this became a regular habit, the camp became their territory, and they would react every time a stranger or other animal came close to the camp. The humans began to accept the presence (and usefulness) of the scavengers and would not drive them away.

The more confident wolves were most likely the ones to approach the humans and even break away from their pack to live among them. The humans soon learned that wolves could track game and slow it down until they could appear with axes or spears, and later, bows and arrows. The wolves began to assist man in hunting, act as cleanup detail, provide warmth, and, yes, serve as food. They may have even let humans help raise their puppies.

In time, this incredible emerging species, known now as *Canis familiaris* (or "the dog"), adapted to human settlements, developed a tame disposition, and became trainable. As society became agriculture based, early man learned to develop herding skills in his dogs. Others were bred to pull plows, retrieve birds during hunts, or serve religious functions.

Because dogs no longer had to bring down large prey, they developed smaller skulls and teeth. They began wagging their tails and developing multicolored coats. At some point, humans began to accelerate the process of domestication by choosing dogs based on juvenile traits such as playful behavior, large eyes, and rounded heads.

Because domestic dogs don't live in the wild and hunt for food, they can exhibit variations in size and shape that not only affect functions such as breathing and chewing, but would have once led to their extinction. As anyone with a Maltese will know by now, some breeds exist because of survival of the cutest!

Dogs are thought to have evolved from wolves through thousands of years of human domestication.

HISTORY OF THE MALTESE

The exact origin of the Maltese—affectionately nicknamed Ye Ancient Dogge of Malta—is unknown. What we do know is that Maltese are among the oldest purebred dogs. They most likely descended from the northern spitz-type dog, which were bred by inhabitants of south-central Europe and what is now Switzerland.

Early Maltese-like dogs eventually made their way south to the Mediterranean region and the ancient trading center of Malta, where they became exotic trade items as well as valuable diplomatic tributes. Their journeys would take them as far as China, where these silky-haired, diminutive dogs were bred with Chinese toy dogs to improve their coat texture and to bring down their size.

The earliest known representations of Maltese are on artifacts found at Fayûm, Egypt, dating as far back as 600 BCE. Effigies of long-haired dogs with flowing ears and curved tails have been unearthed, suggesting the Maltese was one of the breeds worshipped by the Egyptians. Another early image of the Maltese comes from ancient Greece. A Greek vase from around 500 BCE shows a young man walking with what could be a Maltese ahead of him. The inscription above him says, in Greek, "Melitæi."

Ancient Maltese dogs may have helped provide warmth during the cold Italian winters.

WHEN IN ROME...

Known as the Roman Ladies' Dog, Maltese were often carried in the bosoms and sleeves of ancient Roman women. These little dogs were clearly a favorite of the fashionable members of the privileged class. Greek historian Plutarch (46–125 CE) writes, "The Romans lavished so much attention upon spaniels and other pets that Julius Caesar himself complained that the women would do well to give more attention to their offspring and less to the dogs."

Owning a Maltese did have

a practical purpose. In addition to being carried as accessories, they were the ancient equivalent of hot water bottles, extracting pain from delicate stomachs, and may have provided sleeping Romans with warmth during the cold Italian winters. The Romans likely also used their Maltese as watchdogs and let them help keep down the rodent population.

There is a dark side to the Romans' view of dogs and other animals, but we won't go into much detail here. The public shows at the Roman Colosseum are well known. Dogs were used for, well, nutrition, and their hides for clothing. However, many Romans viewed their pets, particularly dogs and birds, as companions whom they personally loved and cared for.

THE MALTESE MAKES ITS MARK IN EUROPE AND ENGLAND

The Maltese was probably brought to England when it was part of the Roman Empire, since the breed was already popular in Rome when Julius Caesar invaded Great Britain around 55 BCE. After the fall of the Roman Empire, however, times were hard for people in Europe. Once again, dogs most likely were bred only to assist man in agriculture and hunting.

The next signs of anything close to the Maltese come from the 13th century, in the form of French paintings, German woodcuts and engravings, and Dutch art. Fourteenth-century French tapestries also depicted the dogs. As people became enlightened once again and the Renaissance blossomed, people began to own and breed dogs for pleasure. Naturalists in the 1500s wrote of Maltese in the homes of the peasants as well as the aristocracy all over Europe.

The Royal Maltese

There are numerous accounts of Maltese living among the royals. Mary, Queen of Scots, is believed to have owned some of the finest specimens of Maltese. Legend tells us of a little white dog who comforted her during her last, tragic moments before she was beheaded in 1587. The dog was said to be found beneath her petticoats after she died. The dog survived but died of a broken heart soon after.

The most celebrated reference to the dog came during the reign of Queen Elizabeth I of England. As her personal physician Dr. John Caius writes in 1570 (translated from Latin in *Toy Dogs and Their Ancestors* by Mrs. Neville Lytton), "There is also among us another kind of highbred dogs . . . those which Callimachus calls Melitei from the Island of Melita in the Sicilian strait, whence that kind chiefly had its origin also. That kind is very small indeed and chiefly sought after for the amusement and pleasure of women. The smaller the kind the more pleasing it is, so that they may carry them in their bosoms, in their beds; and in their arms in their carriages."

In the next century, James VI of Scotland's daughter Elizabeth Stuart, who would become the Winter Queen of Bohemia, was painted with a small white dog resembling a Maltese. As this Elizabeth was the granddaughter of Mary, Queen of Scots, could their dogs have been related? Other European royalty painted with Maltese include Holy Roman Emperor Charles V (1500–1558) and Queen Charlotte of England (1744–1818).

The Maltese found popularity in France as well. In 1798, after Napoléon Bonaparte conquered Malta, one of his first acts as military governor was to select the finest Maltese dog on the island as a gift for his beloved Joséphine.

The Victorian Maltese

For some reason, the Maltese became very scarce in England in the 1830s. In 1841, two Maltese, named Cupid and Psyche, were brought from the Philippines by Captain Lukey of the East India Company as a gift for Queen Victoria. At the end of the nine-month journey, the dogs were too matted and soiled to give to the queen, so he gave them to his brother, a well-known breeder of Mastiffs.

The dogs were bred, and one of the puppies, also named Psyche, was given to a Miss Gibbs, who entered her in a show in Newcastle at Tyne in 1859. According

to *The Dog: In Health and Disease* by John Henry Walsh, when Psyche was at play, she resembled "a ball of animated floss silk, her tail falling on her back like spun glass." Three years later, 20 Maltese were entered in a show in London. Many more Maltese would be brought from the Philippines over the next few years, undoubtedly descendants of the dogs traded centuries before between China and the Mediterranean region.

Queen Victoria did end up with at least one Maltese—her much-beloved Chico. Several of her Maltese were photographed in 1896 for the *Ladies' Kennel Journal*.

The Maltese Coat

In the 19th century, the Maltese was commonly called the "shock dog." This was not due to static from the coat, although that happens! "Shock" comes from the mid–17th century word "*shough*," which means a shaggy breed of lapdog.

The Maltese *were* pretty unkempt. Bathing was not a common custom among people in those days, so it is unlikely they bathed the dogs. The Maltese coat was curlier then, too, as depicted in paintings and drawings of the time. Because the breed was not necessarily pure, the influence of Bichons, Havanese, and Poodles would have made the coat curlier and maybe even thicker than we see today.

Back then, it was common to trim Maltese dogs to make them look like lions. The body coat was shaved from the rear quarters to the ribs. The legs and tail, except for the pompoms, were shaved as well. There was a large mane around the ribs, neck, and head, much like the modern Poodle clip. These Maltese "lion dogs" appeared in many paintings of the period.

Another theory as to the origin of the term "lion dog" is a strange one! Italian naturalist Ulisse Aldrovandi (1522–1605) claimed that if a Maltese about to have puppies was allowed to sleep on sheepskin, the puppies were born with longer coats and manes more lion-like than if she slept on straw. The things we learn from the past!

THE THOROUGHLY MODERN MALTESE

In 1873, the Kennel Club was founded in England, and its first studbook featured 24 registered Maltese. The descendants of Cupid and Psyche were owned by a prominent breeder of the time, Lady Giffard, whose dogs were noted for their long, silky coats. Because of her influence, Cupid and Psyche are believed to be the ancestors of a majority of Maltese dogs in Great Britain and the United States.

In the early 20th century, the Kennel Club allowed "Maltese dogs, other than white" to enter its dog shows under a separate breed class. Some dogs were light brown, others all black or white with colored markings—the more color, the better. Colored Maltese were common in England and Europe at the time. Their ancestry often could not be traced, but they obviously came from past matings to Poodles, Pomeranians, and other breeds.

THE MALTESE IN AMERICA

Breeding and show records were sparse during the early days of American Maltese. The first Maltese registered in the United States was white with black ears. This glamorous pioneer was shown at the Westminster Kennel Club's 1879 Third Annual New York Bench Show of Dogs as a Maltese Skye Terrier. Westminster's first all-white Maltese was shown two years earlier at their First Annual New York Bench Show of Dogs as a Maltese Lion Dog.

Maltese were first shown in the American Kennel Club's (AKC) Miscellaneous Class, meaning they could not compete for championship points. (This is the normal procedure for new breeds to determine if there is enough nationwide interest in the breed.) Maltese were eventually moved to the Non-Sporting Group and then the Toy Group, where they remain today. AKC studbook registrations

Many of today's Maltese descended from the 19th-century dogs Cupid and Psyche, who were originally intended as gifts for Queen Victoria.

were originally made on the basis of dog show wins as opposed to breeding records. The first official Maltese registrations in the AKC studbook were Snips and Topsy, pedigree unknown, in 1888. The first champion was Thackery Rob Roy in 1901, owned by Mrs. C. S. Young.

The American Maltese Association (AMA)

The American Maltese Association (AMA) was founded in 1961, with origins back to 1906, when it was known as the Maltese Terrier Club of America. That organization became the National Maltese Club and held its first specialty show at the Waldorf Astoria Hotel in New York in 1917. After several more changes, representatives of two clubs, the Maltese Dog Club of America and the Maltese Dog Fanciers of America, met at the Henry Hudson Hotel in New York City in 1961 to form one united club, and the American Maltese Association was created. Eight years later, it became the American Kennel Club's official parent club for the Maltese.

The AMA aims to encourage and promote quality breeding of the Maltese. There are more than 250 members across the country and some international members as well. A national specialty show is held annually, with conformation, obedience, and rally events, an awards banquet, seminars, parties, and lots of fun. The AMA celebrated its 50th anniversary with a specialty held in Lombard, Illinois, in 2015.

CHARACTERISTICS OF YOUR MALTESE

Very few dog breeds have remained as true to type throughout the centuries as the Maltese. Though coat texture and color have varied (and even the size has, somewhat), the overall look of the Maltese is recognizable in art from as back far as 2,800 years ago. That is a remarkable claim! Perhaps 19th-century author Hugh Dalziel said it best in *British Dogs: Their Varieties, History, Characteristics, Breeding, Management, and Exhibition*: "They are little animated heaps of pure white glistening silk."

PHYSICAL CHARACTERISTICS OF THE MALTESE

Breeds recognized by the American Kennel Club (AKC) have a breed standard, a written description of what the ideal specimen of the breed would be. Dog show judges evaluate an individual dog against this standard, rather than against other dogs in the ring. The standard is originally written by the parent club, in this case the American Maltese Association (AMA), and then approved by the AKC.

In addition to the standard, dogs are judged by *type*. This quality is a little trickier because it is even more subjective. Type is what, at first glance, separates that breed from all other breeds, such as its behavior, appearance, and carriage.

Following is a description of the ideal Maltese as per the AMA breed standard. Remember, there is no such thing as the perfect dog, not even the best of champions. If your little Maltese does not seem to meet this standard, he is still more than worthy of your love and affection! Just let him do what he does best—be cute!

Phrases in italics taken from the most recent AMA breed standard (1964).

GENERAL APPEARANCE

The Maltese is a toy dog covered from head to foot with a mantle of long, silky, white hair. This startlingly white hair distinguishes the Maltese coat from the white, curly-coated Bichon Frise and the silky-coated Havanese, which can be any color and have any markings. This silky white coat is an example of breed type, a trait that separates Maltese from other breeds.

He is gentle-mannered and affectionate, eager and sprightly in action, and, despite his size, possessed of the vigor needed for the satisfactory companion. Maltese tend to be on duty at all times, ready to cheer us up, keep us entertained, or simply be there for us if that is all we ask. This is likely the attribute that has attracted men, women, and children to this delightful breed for millennia.

According to their breed standard, Maltese make affectionate, sprightly companions.

HEAD

Of medium length and in proportion to the size of the dog. Just as it sounds, the head should not be too big or too small.

The **skull** *is slightly rounded on top, the stop moderate.* By rounded, we mean the top of the head should not be apple-shaped. This rounded head is a look the Maltese has in common with many of the Asian breeds it shares ancestry with. The stop is the indentation between the skull and nasal bone, below the eyes. You don't want the angle of the stop to be strong, as on a Bulldog.

The drop **ears** *are rather low set and heavily feathered with long hair that hangs close to the head.* If the ears are set too high, like on a terrier, the hair will not hang close to the head.

Eyes *are set not too far apart; they are very dark and round, their black rims enhancing the gentle yet alert expression.* This is an extremely important trait of the Maltese. The eyes should not be too deep-set, and they should not bulge. These characteristics will affect the dog's expression. The black rims indicate good pigment. It is even better if the dog has what we call halos, which are defined as the darkening of the skin around the eyes, like smudged eye liner. Although this is not mentioned in the breed standard, it is a plus.

Note: The term "black points" is used to refer to the black pigment on the eye rims, nose, and toe pads.

The **muzzle** *is of medium length, fine and tapered but not snipy. The nose is black.* If the muzzle is too long or too broad, it will take away from the delicate features of the face. "Snipy" means too pointed; this is another common fault. A dark black nose indicates good pigment.

The teeth meet in an even, edge-to-edge **bite**, *or in a scissors bite.* With a scissors bite, the upper incisors (front four teeth) are located in front of the lower incisors when the mouth is closed.

NECK

Sufficient length of neck is desirable as promoting a high carriage of the head. In other words, a long neck (but not too long!) will carry the beautiful head proudly.

BODY

Compact, the height from the withers to the ground equaling the length from the withers to the root of the tail. This means cobby, or square. The withers is the point on the dog's shoulders that is highest. Today's Maltese remains in many ways the same as the perfectly proportioned dog described by Aristotle 23 centuries ago. *Shoulder blades are sloping, the elbows well knit and held close to the body. The back is level in* **topline**, *the ribs well sprung.* The topline is the spinal section from the top of the shoulder blades to the end of his tail root. It would be undesirable, for example, for the rear part of the topline to be higher than the shoulders. *The chest is fairly deep, the loins taut, strong, and just slightly tucked up underneath.*

TAIL

A long-haired plume carried gracefully over the back, its tip lying to the side over the quarter. Nearly all the depictions of the Maltese throughout the centuries have featured that tail carried over the back, originating from the early spitz dogs. "Over the quarter" refers to the tail lying within the back one-fourth of the dog, as opposed to what is called a "gay tail," which is curved over the back. A tail that is too tightly curled is a fault as well.

LEGS AND FEET

Legs are fine-boned and nicely feathered. The Maltese standard is one of the few to mention this trait, so it is important. Feathered simply means "has long hair." *Forelegs are straight, their pastern joints well knit and devoid of appreciable bend. Hind legs are strong and moderately angulated at stifles and hocks. The feet are small and round, with toe pads black.* Occasionally you will see pink toe pads. This is not crucial and certainly does not affect the dog, but they should be black. *Scraggly hairs on the feet may be trimmed to give a neater appearance.*

COAT AND COLOR

The coat is single, that is, without undercoat. It hangs long, flat, and silky over the sides of the body almost, if not quite, to the ground. The long head-

Maltese puppies often have tan or lemon coloring on their ears, but this usually fades as they mature.

hair may be tied up in a topknot or it may be left hanging. Any suggestion of kinkiness, curliness, or woolly texture is objectionable. In the past 100 years, dedicated breeders have worked to eliminate these textures that are genetically in common with Poodles, Bichons, and other related breeds.

Color, pure white. Light tan or lemon on the ears is permissible, but not desirable. This light tan and lemon are evidence of the colored Maltese of the past. Puppies often have this lemon coloring, but it usually fades as they mature. As for topknots, puppies are normally shown with a single topknot, adults with two.

Note that the Maltese coat is hair, not fur. Hair tends to be longer and finer in texture, seems to continuously grow, and has a longer growth cycle.

SIZE

Weight is under 7 pounds, with from 4 to 6 pounds preferred. Overall quality is to be favored over size. An 8- or 9-pound (3.5- or 4-kg) Maltese, for example, would not be faulted if he had extremely nice features. As for less than 4 pounds (2 kg), beware of any breeder who uses terms such as "teacup," "micro," and "baby doll" Maltese. Unethical breeders who deliberately downsize their breedings for profit produce dogs with special medical needs, health issues, and shorter life spans.

Occasionally, of course, a dog from a responsible breeding will end up being less than 4 pounds (2 kg) and can be perfectly healthy.

GAIT

The Maltese moves with a jaunty, smooth, flowing gait. Viewed from the side, he gives an impression of rapid movement, size considered. In the stride, the forelegs reach straight and free from the shoulders, with elbows close. Hind legs to move in a straight line. Cowhocks or any suggestion of hind leg toeing in or out are faults. These terms relate to structural faults that would detract from a smooth, effortless movement, such as causing bouncing, shorter stride, crabbing (moving with the body at an angle to the front), etc. As Aristotle said all those centuries ago, the Maltese should resemble "a cloud floating through the sky."

TEMPERAMENT

For all his diminutive size, the Maltese seems to be without fear. His trust and affectionate responsiveness are very appealing. He is among the gentlest mannered of all little dogs, yet he is lively and playful as well as vigorous. These traits certainly describe the ideal Maltese and are generally true. But while some Maltese will lavish affection on anyone they meet, others are "one-person dogs." Some are more active and love to play, but others prefer the luxury of a satin pillow. Most Maltese assume that everyone they meet—human or animal—is a friend. Therefore, in order for your Maltese to fulfill his duties as a faithful friend, he should not be shy or aggressive.

LIVING WITH YOUR MALTESE

Dr. Gordon Stables writes in his 1879 book *Ladies' Dogs As Companions: Also a Guide to Their Management in Health and Disease,* "The Maltese doggie seems

Dog Tale

Maltese personalities can certainly vary. Our Nicholas likes to carry a tennis ball to the top of his little ramp, let it roll down, and retrieve it, only to repeat the exercise until he gets bored. Toby demands to be picked up at random times, and you don't dare ignore him or he becomes indignant, snorting and stomping. Tinkerbell prefers to lounge on her antique doll bed, although she does like to play hide-and-seek.

to possess the gift of knowing friend from foe. He is a very lively little lad as well, and funny, quite bewitching in fact. I defy anyone not to be amused at his winning wee ways."

Day-to-day life with the Maltese is truly a joy. If he sleeps in your bed, he will likely awaken you in the morning by kissing your face, eager to start his adventures. If you are having a lazy day, he will be happy to lounge on the couch with you—usually on the back cushions. If this is a day for a walk in the park, he will enjoy that, too. Generally speaking, Maltese can have a lot of energy and require a lot of human attention. They are clearly at our beck and paw!

COMPANIONABILITY WITH OTHER DOGS

Your Maltese will be meeting other dogs throughout his lifetime. You may even have a dog already. A good idea is to introduce them on neutral ground. Choose a place where neither dog is likely to feel territorial. Perhaps they could meet somewhere in the neighborhood or at the pet supply store and then go home together. Be positive so that your dogs will not sense any nervousness on your part. Most likely they will try to play, so let them sniff and praise them for any positive behavior. Then take them home. Make sure you have put away the first dog's toys and bowls so that they don't become a source of conflict. Dogs already

If you have another dog, introduce him to your new Maltese on neutral ground and praise both dogs for positive behavior.

present in the household tend to accept puppies more readily than another adult, but why risk it?

Plan activities for both dogs, such as a walk in the park. Try to give them equal attention and quality time with you. Continue to monitor their prized possessions, though. They may have to play with their favorite toys in separate rooms. And it may be necessary to feed them in separate areas.

As for meeting dogs away from home, you will just have to decide on a case-by-case basis. You won't want to take a chance on a large dog injuring your little one, even if the injury occurs in play. Sometimes it is better just to pick your Maltese up and avoid the situation. If the dog you meet is also a toy, let them sniff each other and see if they want to be friends. If you are unsure, just keep the greetings short and praise your boy for a nice hello as you keep moving. If either dog chooses to be rambunctious, remove your Maltese from the situation immediately.

COMPANIONABILITY WITH CATS

If you have a cat in the household, let the cat and your new Maltese check each other out at a distance with the dog on a leash or the cat in his carrier. Talk to and pet your dog, getting him relaxed. Give both animals a treat. Repeat these short visits several times a day. Once they get along during leashed visits, try with the dog unleashed (and the cat free) until they accept each other. Don't leave them alone until you are certain they are friends, and make sure they each have their own space.

COMPANIONABILITY WITH CHILDREN

Look back to your childhood and you will probably recall that having a pet was one of the most joyful times of your young life. Dogs can teach children about responsibility, compassion, and how to care for another being.

Before adopting or buying a Maltese, however, consider the ages and maturity levels of the children in the household. Due to their size and fragile nature, Maltese generally are not recommended for very young children. The child would not hurt or scare him intentionally, but if the dog is accidentally dropped or fallen on, it could be disastrous.

Older children, however, will find great joy in taking care of this confident, playful dog. Teaching a child the safe way to treat a Maltese is the best way to ensure that their relationship stays healthy as long as they are together. And teaching your Maltese that children are not to be feared will lessen the chance he will ever threaten a child or end up in a shelter.

Older children find great joy in taking care of the confident, playful Maltese.

Meeting the Children

First of all, keep in mind that we tower over these little dogs—even children do. So with everyone sitting on the floor, let the puppy run back and forth among the humans, encourage him, introduce him to his toys, and so on. Be silly and your Maltese will double the silliness in return. They are charming, playful, and mischievous little dogs. Let that personality flourish!

Once the dog and child feel comfortable together, talk about boundaries. Explain to the child that she must pet the dog only after he has seen and smelled her hand. Then she can pet gently. Tell her not to pull on the dog's ears or tail, poke him, step on him, or otherwise put the dog in danger. Make sure the child knows not to leave the dog where he can jump off furniture and hurt himself. This is a good time to teach the child that animals are living, breathing beings worthy of respect. As much as the Maltese looks like a beautiful stuffed animal, he can never be mistaken for one. The best way to educate your children is through example.

You can teach your child puppy safety by having her help you keep dangerous objects such as small children's toys and food out of the dog's reach. Another consideration with small children is to make sure they know how to prevent the dog from accidentally escaping through the door. Your curious Maltese may walk out the front door with no regard for what dangers may lurk outside.

Once the child understands the dog's needs, she can share in the responsibilities of feeding, providing water for, walking, and even grooming the dog. Taking care of and loving a dog can be the most wonderful experience of a child's young life.

THE HYPOALLERGENIC DOG?

Maltese, along with a number of other breeds, are typically thought to be hypoallergenic because they produce less dander and saliva and shed less than other dogs. But are these breeds really hypoallergenic? There is no easy answer to this.

A 2011 study by Henry Ford Hospital in Michigan evaluated whether homes of hypoallergenic dogs have a lower level of allergens than homes with dogs who are known to shed dander. Unfortunately, they found no scientific basis to this claim.

On the other hand, or paw, a University of Wisconsin–Madison pediatrician conducted a number of studies that demonstrated that having a pet in the home can actually lower a child's likelihood of developing related allergies by as much as 33 percent. The research showed that children exposed early on to animals tend to develop stronger immune systems overall. Of course, this does not help adults already struggling with allergies. Allergy shots to build up a tolerance to the pet dander are always an option. (They work!)

This is not to say it is impossible to have a Maltese if you have allergies. If you bathe him frequently and keep him dutifully brushed, this will cut down on the amount of dander. A short "puppy clip" haircut will be easier to manage. Wipe his face with a damp cloth after he eats to keep the hair clean and use a towel to keep the whiskers dry.

Although Maltese have magnificent coats, they can get sunburned, so don't let your pup become overexposed.

THE ALL 'ROUND DOG

A Maltese is happy in a small apartment, on a farm (yes!), or jet-setting around the world. He is quite content napping on his satin pillow while the family relaxes. He will enjoy going out with you in his carrier or stroller so that he can be lavished with attention at the pet supply store or the park. He thrives on warm weather and will come running back inside when the ground is snow-covered.

The Maltese loves to play outside. Although he is a coated breed, that pink skin can get sunburned, so don't let him become overexposed. And never leave him alone in his yard, even if the yard is securely fenced. There could be dangers lurking, such as biting insects, toxic mulch, or even low-flying predator birds, such as hawks or owls. Of course, he should *never* be tethered!

Though the Maltese is too small to confront an intruder, his love for barking makes him an excellent watchdog. Try to contain that barking instinct if you live in an apartment, however, or it could become nuisance barking.

EXERCISE REQUIREMENTS

All dogs need some exercise for bone and joint health, just as humans do. Exercise improves heart and lung function and allows the dog to rest more peacefully at

Daily exercise is a must to keep your Maltese in shape both physically and mentally.

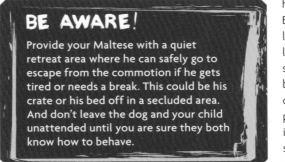

home—and not get bored! Boredom in a breed as lively as a Maltese could lead to problem behaviors such as digging, excessive barking, chewing, and destruction. Daily walks, playtime, or other exercise is a must to keep him in shape both physically and mentally. He will be all the better for it!

You can keep your Maltese exercised indoors by playing hide-the-food games or using food-stuffable toys. A Maltese is small enough to play fetch indoors. Just avoid games like tug-of-war that can get too rough and injure your dog's mouth or make him aggressive.

TRAINABILITY

Maltese respond well to training and can be taught a variety of entertaining tricks and commands. They are quick learners with a strong desire to please, and many standard obedience commands can be taught right inside your house.

Like many toy breeds, Maltese can be difficult to housetrain. Perhaps a small dog gets away with behavior the owner would never tolerate in a larger dog. A "little piddle" from a puppy may not be a big deal to human observers or may even be overlooked. Often owners feel reluctant to put such a cute little puppy in a crate for crate training. However, he is still a D-O-G and needs to be treated as such in certain circumstances. (But don't tell him that!) Allowing a puppy to run free in the house is a mistake many people make. This may inadvertently encourage the puppy to continue having "accidents."

It is definitely possible to housetrain a Maltese. You simply must be consistent with your methods and not give in to cuteness. You will be happy you did! Maltese have long life expectancies, with an average life span of 15 years or more. So taking the time to train him pays off with years of living with a well-mannered companion.

SUPPLIES FOR YOUR MALTESE

Part of the fun of adopting a new dog is the preparation, whether you are expecting a puppy or an adult. Besides the obvious supplies such as food, bowls, collars, and leashes, there is a huge array of doggy delights you can buy for the elegant, sophisticated Maltese!

BABY GATES

Baby gates can be lifesavers for your puppy or adult until he learns about his new home. You will want to keep him confined to an area where he will be safe from stairs, doors that open to the outside, and rooms that are not yet dog-proof. A confined area also makes housetraining easier.

Now, a word about gates. Maltese are escape artists! For this reason, avoid accordion gates. The V-shaped openings along the top can pose a strangulation hazard. They are just as dangerous for a dog as they are for children. Mesh gates or solid gates are much safer, and those with vertical bars are harder for your little monkey to climb. Vertical gates made of PVC pipe are pretty foolproof. They are permanently attached at the sides and swing open.

BEDS

If you want to make your Maltese feel right at home in the style of the ancients, follow this advice from *The Deipnosophists* by Athenaeus of Naucratis (3rd century CE): "Strew, then, soft carpets underneath the dog, and place beneath cloths of Milesian wool; and put above them all a purple rug." Or you could go to your local pet store and see what they have.

You can find every size, shape, color, and fabric imaginable for a dog bed. Some are merely functional; others are just plain adorable. That is probably what you will want for your little Maltese. Look for beds that are washable or have washable covers and will fit in a standard washing machine. Satin and other smooth materials are coat-friendly. Denim and corduroy are durable. And the better made, the less likely your dog will find a seam or tear that will cause inexplicable amounts of stuffing to escape onto your floor!

CLOTHING

It might be hard to resist that little polka-dotted jumper for your female Maltese. Or for a male, a little sailor suit to depict his seafaring heritage. Halloween is notorious for all kinds of little canine monsters and angels. And don't forget a raincoat to keep that silky coat dry. But is dressing your dog the right thing to do?

It all depends on how you wish to spend time with your dog and whether it makes the dog happy. Maltese in general thrive on attention from their owners no

matter how it comes. They love going out in public and having strangers make a fuss over them. Yet other dogs complain even while being fitted for a basic collar.

Sadly, so many dogs suffer abuse and loneliness. They would love any type of attention. So find a happy medium. Spend quality time with your Maltese, and if it makes him happy to wear a coat or some faux fur, what is the harm?

As winter approaches, clothing may *not* be optional. Maltese are single-coated and very susceptible to cold, especially if they are very young, ill, or elderly. A nice warm sweater or coat, and maybe even little boots, will be much appreciated.

COLLARS AND LEASHES

Toy dogs carried in the arms of the Roman ladies were draped with gold chains, semi-precious gems, and pearls as a sign of affluence. This opulence continued through the Renaissance and reached its height in the early 1900s in New York, Paris, and London, where dressmakers specialized in posh canine garments featuring embroidered monograms and Valenciennes lace. Designers were even reviewed by fashion critics with the same jargon used for women's attire.

We still put a lot of thought into which collar to select, and if we wish to adorn our Maltese like the ancients did, there are certainly enough options on the market! But we can keep it simple during puppyhood.

There isn't a lot of size difference between a puppy and adult collar, so if it is adjustable, you will probably be able to use it for a long time. The collar should be tight enough not to slip over his head but not so tight as to irritate the skin or, of course, choke him! You should be able to fit one or two fingers between the neck and the collar. Remember to check it at least once or twice a week as the puppy grows.

Nylon collars cause the least damage to the silky Maltese coat. Even better are the rolled nylon collars for minimal coat damage. Matching nylon leashes 3/8 inches (1 cm) wide and 4 to 6 feet (1.2 to 1.8 m) in length are best. Thin leather leashes are good for training—they are easier on the hands—but may be too heavy for everyday use with such a small dog.

Your Maltese's collar should be tight enough not to slip over his head but not so tight that it's uncomfortable.

BE AWARE!

For dogs with delicate tracheas like the Maltese, choke chain collars simply are not safe, and the links could catch the hair and pinch the dog. Leaving a dog in a crate with such a collar could cause the end loop to become caught in the floor grate and choke the dog. Pinch or prong collars should never be used.

Retractable leads seem like a good idea but are somewhat controversial. A dog can dart away, causing the leash to reel to its full length and jerk the dog by the neck. If you are not paying attention, he could pull the leash far enough to get in harm's way. Another factor is that your dog may never learn to walk by your side if he is permitted to run ahead of you.

Your designer Maltese will, of course, expect only the most stylish materials and designs. Consider what theme you would like to convey—glamorous, preppy, bones and paw prints, even seasonal. How about black velvet with Swarovski crystals—all the rage!

CRATES

Using a crate to housetrain your dog is universally recognized as the best way to achieve your goals. It may seem unfair at first, but your Maltese should eventually see the crate as a safe haven. A crate is also a good place to keep your dog if people will be going in and out of your house so that he doesn't get loose. Crate training will be discussed later, but for now, let's see how to shop for a suitable crate.

A crate should be at least twice as large as the grown dog so that there will be room for his water, bed, and toys and he will not feel cramped. Wire or nylon mesh crates give your dog more access to his surroundings, but a wire crate has the drawback of catching his hair in the wire. Plastic airline-type crates offer more privacy but may be hotter or seem confining. If you can find a crate with a divider so that the area can be made smaller while he is a puppy, that would be ideal. Crates are a good way to transport your dog, so portability is a consideration as well. Of course, you can buy custom-made crates that double as fashionable furniture, such as occasional tables, nightstands, and armoires. Not portable but certainly worthy of a Maltese!

EXERCISE PENS

An exercise pen can be made large enough for your dog's bed, toys, water, and piddle pads, plus a play area. Most can be purchased in panels to make the area as large as you like. Some panels have small doors for the dogs. Most exercise pens have an optional top panel.

Our little escape artist, Nicholas, never injured himself escaping from his exercise pen, but he could have. A Maltese can be seriously hurt falling down

Dog Tale

Exercise pens made of PVC pipe are about the best you can buy. They are easy to clean and virtually escape-proof—except for our Maltese Nicholas, that is. We couldn't figure out how he was using the slippery vertical rails to get out. Then we caught him in the act. He was bunching up his plush bed high enough to climb up and jump out. Watch these little guys! They are escape artists.

steps or off furniture. So carefully look over your little dog's surroundings and make sure he is free from peril. Pens made of PVC pipes are probably the hardest to escape from.

While we are on the subject of escaping, check your fence perimeter to ensure there are no holes or gaps in the fence that he can wiggle through and make sure your fence's gate will latch safely. If you are unable to see the gate from the door, you may want to put a lock on it so that no one will leave it open.

FOOD AND WATER BOWLS

There are so many types of bowls available, ranging from stainless steel to hand-painted ceramic. (Check to make sure any painted bowls do not contain lead-based paint.) Some bowls are on pedestals; others can be elevated as needed. An elevated bowl will keep your little one's face drier and tidier when he drinks or eats.

Avoid plastic bowls. Some health care professionals feel the plastic can harbor bacteria and cause an inflammation or breakout on your dog's muzzle or inside his mouth. Besides, plastic bowls are usually flimsy and easy to knock over. Regardless of your choice of bowl, a cute placemat will protect your floor and make cleanup a lot easier.

There is evidence that the minerals in tap water can cause stains on light-

Considering a ceramic bowl for your Maltese? Check to make sure that it doesn't contain lead-based paint.

colored hair and even increase the occurrence of tearstains after the water is ingested. Therefore, some people prefer to give their Maltese bottled, distilled, or filtered water. Another option for the Maltese to keep his face dry is a water bottle. You can hang one inside his crate or buy a freestanding one. Make sure he is able to get enough water drinking this way and has access to fresh, clean water at all times.

GROOMING SUPPLIES

Prepare yourself! Compared to other breeds, the Maltese needs a lot of grooming equipment. A more specific list of grooming items will be discussed later, but this is what you will need for a start.

COMBS

The best type of comb to use is a Greyhound comb. Originally made for the textile industry in England (and not for Greyhound dogs), these combs are static-free and last forever. They may not be available at a basic pet supply store. If not, look for a metal comb, either with a handle or not—whatever feels best in your hand. You will also need a good-quality steel pin brush.

FASHION ACCESSORIES

To make topknots, use small latex bands like those an orthodontist would give you for braces. They come in all colors and are easier on the hair than ordinary rubber bands. Latex bands can be purchased online or at a dog show. Small fabric-covered scrunchies are also nice. Note: Like some humans, dogs can be allergic to latex. Although this is rare, watch out for skin irritation near where the bands are used.

And bows. Lots of bows. For the show ring, Maltese puppies wear one topknot with a bow. Adults wear two topknots with very small bows, less than 1/2 inches (1.3 cm) wide. You may find, like I do, that the single topknot is cuter and easier for around the house. We will talk more about bows in the grooming chapter.

SHAMPOO

As with human hair, sometimes it takes a few tries to find the right shampoo for your Maltese. You will need a shampoo for a single-coated breed, preferably with whitener. Too much whitener can cause dry hair, and some shampoos can cause coarseness. Talk to your dog's breeder about which shampoo to use for your dog's coat texture.

SHEDDING CLEANUP

Although Maltese do not shed like short-coated breeds, there will be errant hairs on you and some dust bunnies around the house. Pick up a lint roller (and plenty of refills) or use duct tape wrapped around your hand for your clothing.

HARNESSES

Harnesses are a secure way to walk your dog without putting pressure on his neck. Just make sure your dog's harness fits correctly and does not chafe under the front legs. Rather new on the clothing scene are little coats with built-in harnesses with a loop for attaching the leash. These coats are stylish and secure.

IDENTIFICATION

Nothing is more frightening than the realization that your dog has run out of the door or has loosened from his leash. It is *imperative* that your dog have a means of identification.

The first thing to do is check to see if your city and county require that you license your dog. You may need a tag for the dog's collar, not only to prove he has been registered but to help in returning him to you. Some municipalities limit the number of dogs you may have. It's always a good idea to check out the local laws on dog ownership and responsibilities before acquiring your dog.

MALTESE

Another safety measure is to place rescue stickers in your window or door to alert firefighters and other responders that there is a dog or other pet in your house or apartment. These little stickers can save your pets' lives in the event of a fire or other disaster.

Always keep current photos of your Maltese based on his age and coat length. These will be invaluable if your dog becomes lost.

COLLAR TAGS

A pet supply store, a vet's office, or an online service can make a metal tag with everything you need to identify your dog. This is as important as any other pet supply. Include your dog's name, your name, and your phone numbers on the tag.

MICROCHIPS

According to the American Kennel Club (AKC), lost pets with microchips are up to 20 times more likely to be returned home. A microchip is implanted by your vet or at a microchip clinic offered at a dog show or other dog event. The chip, which is about the size of a grain of rice, is usually implanted between the shoulder blades and is read by a scanner.

You will then fill out the form provided by the vet, including your name, phone numbers, and emergency contacts, and send it to the AKC for enrollment in its database. (Be sure to send in the paperwork or your dog will not be enrolled.) If you move or change phone numbers, don't worry. You can make updates at any time.

If your Maltese accidentally slips out the door or breaks away from his lead at the park, anyone who finds him can take him to a veterinarian to have the microchip scanned. The AKC will then begin contacting your emergency e-mails and phone numbers so that you can plan to be reunited with your pet. Most animal shelters will also routinely scan any dog turned in as lost.

PET CARRIER OR BAG

Consider using a pet carrier or airline bag for bringing a wiggly puppy or adult home. It is not safe to hold a dog on your lap in the car, particularly when you are in

PUPPY POINTER

Maltese are very bright, so you have to be consistent. If you feed your puppy once from the table, he will expect it in the future. If you let him play on the bed, he will think it is *his* bed. Decide what kind of adult you want him to be and apply the rules early.

a seat protected by air bags. If your car has front-seat air bags, keep the dog secured in a carrier or airline bag in the back seat. Most carriers have loops to slip seat belts through to secure them in the seat.

Most carriers have loops to slip seat belts through to secure them in the seat.

If you will be traveling frequently by vehicle with your Maltese, consider a plastic crate, as they provide the best protection in case of an accident. If you wish to make a fashion statement, soft-sided carriers of every material and color will keep your dog looking stylish. There are even carriers in the shape and color of little RVs and school buses. If you plan to fly with your Maltese, check airline regulations for permissible sizes.

And for later, don't forget a doggy stroller with a mesh covering so that your dog can see out and get plenty of air. These are especially welcomed by frail or older dogs who can no longer go for a walk.

STEPS AND RAMPS

The Maltese is a very agile and athletic dog. Depending on his size, he may be able to jump on and off your couch (and most likely, will like to lie on the back cushions). Jumping can cause injury to his spine or his knees, however, so it is best to teach him to use little dog steps or a ramp up to your couch and bed. Many companies make these items, or you can custom make one for your pooch. Carpeting will keep his little feet from slipping, so that is a must.

TOYS

Now we're talking! The fun stuff. Let's face it, we will spoil our Maltese. Can you think of a dog more deserving? They return every bit of love given to them with much, much more!

Small latex toys seem to be the most popular items for Maltese. They are generally safe and don't tear easily or break off like vinyl toys can. Small cloth-covered barnyard animals are popular. They are shaped to fit little mouths and are easy to squeak. Plush toys are a favorite of all breeds, but monitor the play at first to make sure your dog does not disembowel the toy. If he is a gentle squeaker, a toy can last for years. Stuffing-free toys are great, especially the ones that make a strange crinkly noise.

Dogs are partially color-blind, most likely seeing yellow, violet, and blue extremely well. You may want to consider these colors if you plan to play with your Maltese in the grass. Although red, orange, and green are standout colors to us, your dog will probably see them as shades of dull gray. Or he may just like the squeak or the ease of carrying a toy around, regardless of color!

Although rawhide is popular, it is not ideal for the Maltese. It becomes soggy and sticky and can cause discoloration around the mouth and paws. Furthermore, since rawhide is not regulated by the FDA, it can contain lead, mercury, or even salmonella. It can also swell within the digestive tract. The same applies to other agriculture products, such as cow hooves and pig ears. Besides, Maltese are too sophisticated for such things!

Plush toys are a favorite of all breeds. With gentle dogs, they can last for years.

FEEDING YOUR MALTESE

Toy breeds require more calories per pound (0.5 kg) than larger dogs do.

I f you wish to feed your Maltese like the ancient Greeks, *The Deipnosophists* by Athenaeus of Naucratis gives feeding instructions for the dog of a mythological princess: "In goose's milk / Soak him some groats." Should your grocery store be out of these ingredients, you may have to opt for a more modern diet.

Toy breeds have different nutritional needs than large dogs. They require more calories per pound (0.5 kg) and have smaller stomachs. This is why most foods for small dogs are higher in calories than large-breed diets and more concentrated with higher protein and fat levels.

THE BALANCED DIET

Every cell in our bodies and those of our pets depends on what we consume. With your Maltese eating such small portions of food, you want to make every morsel count. Following is an explanation of the major food components so that we can see what we need to look for in a food.

CARBOHYDRATES

Carbohydrates are fuel sources transformed into sugars as they digest. One of these sugars is glucose, the body's chief source of energy. Starchy carbohydrates add structure, texture, and form to dry food and are relatively inexpensive. Most commercial dry dog foods contain between 30 percent and 70 percent carbohydrates.

Carbohydrates can be nutritional or non-nutritional. Sources of nutritional carbohydrates include corn, rice, wheat, barley, and oats. Non-nutritional carbohydrates, such as pectin, gum, mucilage, and cellulose, are known as "fibers" and are used to provide bulk. Make sure there are fewer non-nutritional carbohydrates, or they could dilute the other ingredients.

Many dog foods are now labeled "grain-free." Grains are a great source of energy and a good source of protein when blended with an animal protein such as chicken. Unless your dog is allergic to one or more grains, there is no reason to avoid them.

FATS

Dogs can manufacture fats internally, but some fats need to be ingested in the diet. Fat is stored in a reservoir which insulates, cushions, and gives shape to the dog's body. Excess ingested fat and carbohydrates are stored in this fat reservoir and are withdrawn as needed. A good balance of these fats will help your Maltese's skin and coat.

Good sources of fat are chicken and other poultry, beef, pork, lamb, and fish oils. Fats in the form of oils derived from plants such as soybean, flaxseed, and safflower are also good sources.

Two essential fatty acids are omega-3 and omega-6 fatty acids. These are included in many dog foods and supplements because of their known health effects, including reducing inflammation, improving cognitive function, and improving neurological development.

Too much of the wrong fats are thought to cause, or at least provoke, pancreatitis, especially in small dogs like the Maltese. Sometimes attacks occur after the dog has eaten the wrong foods. Signs of a pancreatitis attack are vomiting, diarrhea, and a painful abdomen. This is a veterinary emergency!

PROTEINS

Proteins are vital for all aspects of growth and development and the structural makeup of the immune system. They are burned as calories and can be converted to and stored as fat. They also produce hormones, enzymes, and other bodily secretions. Proteins are formed by one or more chains of amino acids. Dogs actually require 22 amino acids. They can synthesize 12 of these; the remaining ones—essential amino acids—must be in their food.

The recommended minimum protein content is 18 percent for adult maintenance and 22 percent for growth and reproduction, as established by the Association of American Feed Control Officials (AAFCO). Many toy-breed puppy foods suggest a protein level higher than 22 percent.

VITAMINS

Vitamins are organic substances that are needed in relatively small amounts for growth, fitness, vital processes, and level of activity. Most vitamins cannot be produced by the body and need to be supplied by food. They are either fat soluble (stored in the dog's fatty tissue) or water soluble (excreted if unused).

Oversupplementation causes adverse effects ranging from muscle weakness caused by too much vitamin E to toxicity caused by too much vitamin K, so do not supplement without veterinary supervision. Vitamin deficiencies are rare these days in dogs who are fed quality food. Exceptions may be in young dogs since growth is such a demanding time of life.

MINERALS

Minerals are inorganic compounds required by the body. They need to be supplied to the dog in his food. Minerals commonly added to dog food include calcium, phosphorus, magnesium, sodium, iron, and zinc. Because reactions occur among different minerals in the body, it may be harmful to your dog's health to supplement with minerals that are not needed, so ask your vet before adding any minerals to your dog's diet.

WATER

Water accounts for 60 to 70 percent of the body weight of an adult dog. Water helps regulate body temperature, facilitates the movement of food through the digestive system, and transports other nutrients and oxygen through the blood system to the cells. It is needed for metabolism, to remove toxins, and to provide lubrication for the joints and lung tissues. Losing 15 percent of the body's water content can result in death. This is why your Maltese should always have access to plenty of fresh, clean water.

COMMERCIAL DOG FOOD

In the past, dogs lived off of grains, meats, table scraps, and homemade foods. The thought of trying to provide a dog a balanced diet probably never occurred to even the most meticulous pet owner. Today, dog foods range from breed-specific to disease-specific and come canned, bagged, dehydrated, and frozen. Some products are labeled natural or organic, and include ingredients such as duck, blueberries, and omega-3 fatty acids that are said to promote health. Several companies make foods primarily for toy breeds, so this may be a place to start.

EVALUATING DOG FOODS

The Federal Food, Drug, and Cosmetic Act requires that all animal foods, like human foods, are free of harmful substances, produced under sanitary conditions, safe to eat, and truthfully labeled.

Many pet food regulations are based on a model provided by AAFCO. AAFCO establishes the nutritional standards for complete and balanced pet foods, but it is the responsibility of the pet food company to formulate its products according to the AAFCO standard. The label of a

PUPPY POINTER

Your Maltese puppy has a very high metabolic rate, so feed him calorie-dense food three or four times a day until four months of age so that he doesn't develop hypoglycemia. Hypoglycemia is a condition where blood sugar drops to a dangerously low level in the body.

pet food, as well as its advertising, is highly regulated both on a federal and a state level.

Checking out pet food labels can be daunting, but knowing some basics can help. One important guideline is that ingredients must be listed by weight in descending order. Also keep in mind that though the US Food and Drug Administration (FDA) oversees specific claims on pet food, such as "maintains urinary tract health," "tartar control," and "improved digestibility," terms such as "natural" or "premium" have no official legal or scientific definition. Generally speaking, the fewer ingredients in the food, the healthier it is. Foods with long lists of ingredients usually contain more chemicals and byproducts.

Look for a food with more grain than protein. Also, one or more types of meat should be listed among the first three to five ingredients. Some foods are made primarily of grain and other plant products. These are less expensive, but the quality of the protein may not be as good as it is in meat-based foods. And those that contain a great deal of soy can lead to more stool and flatulence (passing gas), and you don't want that!

DRY VS. CANNED FOOD

Maltese have very small mouths, so their teeth are often crowded, scrambled, and subject to dental problems. Therefore, a dry diet is typically the best choice. Dry diets not only help reduce buildup of tartar and calculus but also promote firmer, healthier stools. Maltese are frequently picky, dainty eaters, so you will want the food to be highly palatable with high digestibility so that your dog will be well nourished. (Low digestibility means that dogs would not be able to absorb all the nutrients from the food, so even food that appears to be high in nutrition may not nourish your Maltese very well if it has low digestibility.) A smaller kibble will be easier to eat.

Canned foods are often made of higher-quality ingredients (particularly meat-based protein) and fewer carbohydrates. Their fats and oils don't easily spoil, because the cans are sealed. Typically there are no artificial flavorings or colorings. And since meat ingredients are closer to their natural state, they are more appetizing. Pets with dental issues or tooth loss may find it easier to chew a softer, canned diet. Note: Don't leave any canned food in your dog's bowl for more than an hour or two, as it can easily go bad. And refrigerate any opened cans.

So which is better? Dry or canned? Our household opts for mixing a spoonful of canned food into the dry kibble to give our Maltese an extra treat.

SEMI-MOIST FOODS

Semi-moist foods, like those in small packets, generally contain a lot of sugar and preservatives. Foods with red dye or beet pulp can stain the coat around the mouth and should be avoided.

SPECIAL DIETS

Special diets are available for nursing mothers, dogs with allergies, dogs with liver or kidney disease, and dogs in other special circumstances. Many of these foods have natural preservatives such as vitamin E rather than chemical preservatives. If your vet determines that your Maltese needs any kind of special diet, make sure that the prescribed regimen is the only food he eats. No unauthorized snacks!

BE AWARE!
You may have heard about numerous dog food recalls over the years. To follow up on recalls or investigate a commercial dog food, visit DogFoodAdvisor.com. You can also sign up to receive e-mails about any recalls. The US Food and Drug Administration's (FDA) website maintains a current list of pet food recalls too.

NONCOMMERCIAL FOODS

"Mrs. Monck feeds her pets nothing but cabbage and rice with just a tiny

If your vet determines that your Maltese needs a special diet, make sure that the prescribed regimen is the only food he eats.

morsel of meat," writes Dr. Gordon Stables in his 1879 book *Ladies' Dogs As Companions: Also a Guide to Their Management in Health and Disease.* Mrs. Monck undoubtedly was doing what she thought best for her Maltese, but today we know more about nutrition. If you wish to cook for your Maltese—yes, some people still do!—there are some factors to consider.

One problem with homemade diets is that the dog owner may have the tendency to increase or decrease ingredients, or will tire of measuring out or slicing an ingredient and simply omit it. If an item is unavailable at the grocer, you need to know what substitution will work or you may throw off the entire diet. For example, low-quality or incomplete proteins could result in poor skin and hair quality, decreased muscle mass, and decreased immune responses. Feeding excess amounts of protein is not likely to be harmful in healthy dogs because the excess is used for energy or is excreted. However, in dogs with renal disease, excess protein may contribute to progression of the disease. A lot of organization is required for a homemade diet, especially if you plan to travel.

Although the idea of cooking for this little guy is appealing and seems extra nurturing, it may be harmful unless done correctly. If you do plan to feed a homemade diet, stay with recipes that have been developed for your dog by your canine nutritionist.

RAW DIET

Proponents of raw diets feel that because dogs evolved to eat animals, not plants, the modern pet dog should do so as well. They claim raw feeding yields better health, cleaner teeth, higher energy, and nicer coats, among other benefits. They point out that racing Greyhounds and sled dogs have been fed raw-meat diets for years. Yet archaeological evidence shows that dogs have eaten both raw and cooked food, as well as any grain-based scraps that came their way, since they befriended man (and woman).

There are two potential problems with the raw diet. First of all, studies have shown that the diets sampled have at least one unacceptably high or low level of some nutrient according to Association of American Feed Control Officials (AAFCO) guidelines. These deficiencies could lead to a serious health problem.

Secondly, raw meat, even that for human consumption, may contain harmful bacteria. Dogs do not seem to be as prone to food poisoning as humans, but puppies, sick dogs, and older dogs could be more susceptible. Raw food may also contain parasites and protozoa that would normally be killed in the manufacturing process. These may put some people at risk; therefore, it is important to thoroughly wash your hands before and after handling the raw foodstuffs. Studies have shown that animals fed raw protein diets shed significantly higher amounts of pathogenic bacteria in their stool than those fed cooked proteins.

A dry diet is typically the best choice for a Maltese.

VEGETARIAN DIET

Dogs are omnivores—that is, they eat both animals and plants.

Therefore, a vegetarian diet may work if you are careful to avoid protein and vitamin deficiencies, especially vitamin B12. You may wish to feed your dog a commercial vegetarian diet that may (or may not) have all of the ingredients needed for a balanced diet. If you decide to feed your dog a vegetarian diet, work with a nutritionist, if possible, and let your vet know.

As for the health benefits, dogs generally do not suffer from coronary artery disease the way humans do, so a vegetarian diet may not have the health benefits you may think it would.

Your author asked several vegetarian friends if they feed their dogs a vegetarian diet. Their response was that, although it was their own dietary choice, they felt their dogs needed meat in their diet. Regardless of personal philosophy, the important thing is not to compromise the health of the dog.

WHEN TO FEED

In ancient times, Maltese were fed tiny portions from golden bowls. Golden bowls may not be practical, but the ancients were right about the small portions—more specifically, small pieces. You want your Maltese to be able to carefully chew his food, as swallowing large pieces may cause stomach problems.

Feed your Maltese puppy three or four times per day to keep his blood sugar from dropping.

Because your Maltese puppy has a very high metabolic rate, feed him calorie-dense food three or four times a day until four months of age so that he doesn't develop hypoglycemia, a drop in blood sugar. After that point, he should be fed at least two meals a day. And unless you want to start a lifelong trend of feeding your Maltese from the table, don't start.

If your Maltese is a slow, picky eater, you may wish to free feed him; that is, leave his food out all day. This will work if he is trained to use a piddle pad or you will be there to hear his pleas to go out, but if this is not the case, feeding this way will likely lead to accidents in the house. Generally, giving your Maltese a limited amount of time to eat solves the problem of finicky eating. He will learn not to miss opportunities or he will feel hungry very soon. Of course, offer him the food again a little later.

Give your dog special snacks of carrots or biscuits made for small breeds at bedtime or when he has been good. Some of these products use beet pulp as a red dye. Stay away from those as they will cause stains on your dog's feet and face and may even contribute to tearstains.

HOW MUCH TO FEED

Because of the breed's high metabolic rate, the Maltese needs to take in more calories per pound (0.5 kg) than other dogs do. These bundles of energy also need the proper nutrition to grow that luxurious coat. A small dog requires 40 calories per pound (0.5 kg) every day, while his large-breed counterpart needs only 22.5 calories per pound (0.5 kg). Combine this with the fact that small dogs have tiny stomachs and you'll see why most foods designed for small breeds are more calorie rich.

As for how much to feed your little guy, the directions on the package are just general guidelines and are usually more than your dog will ever want to eat. The amount and type of food your Maltese needs depends on his activity level, age, build, metabolism, and special health issues. Dogs are individuals, just like people.

An active dog will need more food than a lap dog, and the Maltese can fall into either category. Start with about 25 percent less than the label says and see how that works.

OBESITY

Studies have shown that between 25 and 40 percent of the dogs visiting vet clinics are overweight or obese. Most of these cases are simply due to overfeeding, but occasionally there can be a genetic component or a medical cause such as hypothyroidism. Just as with humans, weight gain in your Maltese is associated with an increased incidence of arthritis, diabetes mellitus, cardiovascular problems, and surgery and anesthesia risks.

A dog is considered obese if he weighs more than 10 to 15 percent above his ideal body weight. So a Maltese who should weigh 5 pounds (2.3 kg) will be obese if he is 1/2 pounds (0.25 kg) overweight! This is hard to imagine but true.

Another way to determine the correct weight is to check your dog's body condition score (BCS). The BCS system rates dogs from "emaciated," where all ribs and lumbar vertebrae along the spine are visible from a distance and the dog has lost body fat and muscle, to "obese," where there are large deposits of fat in most areas and the abdomen is obviously distended.

When you put your hands on your dog's sides, you should be able to feel at least three or four ribs easily. The abdomen should be tucked up when viewed from side and should resemble an hourglass figure from above. Of course, these last two may be difficult if your Maltese has a ton of hair.

WEIGHT-LOSS PROGRAMS

Before starting your Maltese on a weight-loss program, make sure there are no underlying health problems. If your Maltese gets a clean bill of health, your vet can help you calculate the number of calories your dog should eat per day and recommend food that is low in fat and high in protein and nutrients. This is better than simply feeding less food because if you merely reduce portions, your dog will always be hungry and will be getting fewer nutrients.

If you have your Maltese on a weight-loss regimen, here are some things to consider:

• Feed several small meals throughout the day because metabolizing food takes energy.
• Feed low-calorie snacks such as carrots and green beans, but count these treats into the total calories allowed.
• Count in calories from supplements, as some can be rather high in calories.
• Make sure family members and visitors know not to sneak your dog treats.
• Take your dog for walks. This is the best exercise both of you can get. It benefits your body and your mind, and gives you quality time with your little guy.

GROOMING YOUR
MALTESE

The Maltese is a high-maintenance dog whether you keep him in a puppy clip or let his silky hair grow.

The Maltese is a high-maintenance dog whether you keep him in a puppy clip or let his silky hair grow. The amount of grooming you will have to do on an almost daily basis should be a consideration before you buy or adopt this breed. Your Maltese can always go for a spa day once a month for a bath, pedicure, and trim, but his eyes need to be cleaned daily to prevent staining, and like all breeds, his teeth should be brushed at least once a week.

A GOOD TIME TO CHECK YOUR MALTESE

While brushing your Maltese, check for any skin irritation or lumps. Dry, dull skin and brittle hair can be signs of systemic disease or simply the need for a change in food. Check the eyes for discharge. Maltese, especially puppies, often produce tears that can cause clumping at the corner of the eye, and these need to be wiped away. If the discharge seems like too much, it may be a medical issue like dry eye, allergies, or infection.

Check his little button nose. In the winter, many noses lose some pigment due to winter darkness. This is nothing to worry about. The black will return when your Maltese gets back out in the sunshine. Occasionally the nose can appear dry. If so, use some petroleum jelly on his nose for a couple of days and see if

MALTESE

that helps. If it continues to be dry and crusty after a couple days, ask the vet, as it could be related to a dietary problem (or contact dermatitis, if he is using a plastic bowl).

Maltese and other floppy-eared dogs have a tendency toward ear infections. The ears should be clean and pink. If you see a brown or black discharge, it could be ear mites. Redness or swelling could be caused by a yeast infection, which produces a pungent odor. Both of these conditions require medical treatment.

GROOMING SUPPLIES

If you decide to try your hand at grooming your Maltese, here are the items you should have. Even if you send him out to a groomer, you will still need the basics.

- antiseptic ear powder and cleaner
- baby shampoo or face wash for around the eyes
- bows, lots of bows
- latex bands (1/8- or 1/4-inch [0.3- or 0.6-cm]) for the topknot; the type used by orthodontists
- cornstarch, to keep the face dry

Be sure never to leave your Maltese on the grooming table unattended. Falling from this height could hurt his legs or back.

- detangling spray
- flea comb or small cat comb for around the eyes
- good-quality cushion-based steel pin brush
- good-quality trimming scissors
- Greyhound comb or other metal comb with both widely and narrowly spaced teeth
- hair clips
- hair dryer (the kind for pets is best)
- home-perm endpapers
- lint roller and refills
- nail clippers—the guillotine type, the pliers style, or cat nail clippers
- non-slip bath mat
- ratting comb or knitting needle to part hair
- shampoo and conditioner made for a coated breed
- small round-tipped scissors
- spray bottle
- styptic pencil or powder in case of a nail bleed
- tearstain-cleaning solution
- toothbrush and toothpaste made for dogs

You may want to invest in a professional fold-up grooming table to give you a non-slip grooming surface. Another option is a ringside table, a portable version of the grooming table. Be sure never to leave your dog on the table unattended because jumping or falling from this height could hurt his legs or back.

BRUSHING YOUR MALTESE

If you decide to keep your Maltese "in coat," there is a lot of work to do, beginning with preventing mats. To keep your dog in a regular routine, you should brush him at least several times per week. Brushing stimulates blood circulation, and for this reason, can be relaxing for your dog. It also stimulates natural oils and gets rid of loose hair.

You may find out as you go along that you can get by brushing once a week—or you may have to brush daily. Some coats are silkier, some are coarser. Having your Maltese in a puppy clip will not save you from brushing. The shorter clips mat, too, but they *are* easier to maintain.

Grooming should be a positive experience for your Maltese. Use treats as a reward for good behavior and try not to lose patience. He will pick up on your frustration and get agitated, making it even harder to groom him.

HOW TO BRUSH YOUR MALTESE

Now, the routine. It's important to brush every layer of hair, not just the outside layers. If your Maltese is too wiggly, praise him for any progress he makes or offer him a treat every time he lies or stands quietly. It might be a good idea to practice having him lie down without doing any grooming, maybe while rubbing his feet and praising him, until he gets the hang of it.

1. Section off the top layer of coat with hair clips so that you have access to the coat underneath.
2. Using the pin brush, brush the under layer first and then continue until each section is finished.
3. While brushing, lightly mist the coat with the spray bottle to prevent static. The bottle can contain tap water, water mixed with a bit of canine conditioner, or an anti-static dog product. You may prefer to brush the coat out with cornstarch instead.
4. Brush from the skin to *beyond* the end of the hair. If you flip your wrist during the brush stroke, you can break the hair ends.
5. If you find a mat—and you will—sprinkle it with cornstarch or spray it, depending on which method you prefer. Try to separate it with your fingers or use the end tooth of the Greyhound comb. Separating a mat is an art, and

you will soon be a pro once you figure out which grooming tool works best for you. As tempting as it is to just cut out the mat, keep in mind where it is and how it will look once your dog is all groomed and bathed.

PUPPY POINTER

Before you attempt to bathe your Maltese puppy, do a couple of practice sessions. Put your puppy gently in the tub without water. Use a non-slip mat so that he won't slide. Give him a treat and praise him. Before the bath, make sure you have everything at arm's reach— towel, face wash, canine shampoo and conditioner, and a cup to dilute the products, if necessary.

6. When you have finished the dog's back and sides, raise him up, keeping your hand under his front legs and chest to help stabilize him, and comb the hair inside the back legs, on the stomach, and under the front legs. Sometimes it is better to trim small hair clumps on the tender stomach area, as brushing there can really annoy your dog. You may want to trim the area under the tail and around the dog's private area to keep him cleaner.

7. Ears are a prime location for matting. Using a smaller comb, work carefully through the tangled area. This skin here is very delicate, so be gentle.

8. Once all mats have been brushed out, stand your dog up and brush the hair down on both sides. Tidy up the part using the knitting needle or parting comb and give the little guy a break before you tackle the topknots or bath.

BATHING YOUR MALTESE

The key to bathing your Maltese is to bathe him just before he needs it. But how do you know *before* your dog needs his bath? When the coat starts getting dirty, you will see that it is more likely to clump. Then it is too late! You will learn—it will become instinctive.

Selecting the right canine shampoo and conditioner may take some trial and error. A silky-coated Maltese will take less conditioner, for example, than one with a coarser coat. Some breeders like products with whiteners, while others feel they dry out the coat. Whichever shampoo and conditioner you choose, put the bottles in a tub of warm water before the bath so that they will be at a comfortable temperature for your dog. He will appreciate it.

MALTESE

HOW TO BATHE YOUR MALTESE

1. With your Maltese in the tub, saturate the coat with warm water, preferably with a spray hose or cup, and apply the warmed shampoo. Treat the coat as if it were an angora sweater. The more gentle you are with the coat, the fewer tangles you will have later, so no rubbing!
2. Rinse very well.
3. Apply conditioner as directed and let it saturate the coat for a few minutes for optimum benefit. Some conditioners require complete rinsing; some do not.
4. Bundle up your dog in a thick towel and get ready to dry. The sooner you are able to dry your Maltese, the straighter the hair will be.

How Dry He Is

The best dryers come on a stand, leaving your hands free. Pet dryers are preferable, as the heat is milder than that of a human hair dryer. Regardless of which type you use, make sure your Maltese's delicate pink skin does not get too warm and uncomfortable, and never leave your Maltese in a crate with a hair dryer blowing on him. His skin is too delicate for that much heat.

Lay the dog on his side. Clip up the outer layer and dry the undercoat first, brushing it the entire time to keep it straight. Repeat section by section until all the hair is dry. Use an anti-static spray if necessary. Even when you think it is dry enough, dry it more. This is one of the keys to preventing mats. The hair under the ears will take the longest to dry.

Once your dog is thoroughly dry, trim the hair on the feet to give them a rounded appearance. Trim gradually—you can always take more off, but you

> **BE AWARE!**
>
> Maltese are slow to get their adult teeth in. Most breeds start losing baby teeth at three and a half months, while Maltese often don't start until closer to five months. As your puppy's adult teeth come in, he may have difficulty eating due to swollen gums and loose teeth. Soften his food and give him something to chew on to help loosen the teeth. He may enjoy having you massage his gums. Some baby teeth may need to be extracted so that the mouth does not become crowded and ruin the alignment of the teeth.

can't put it back on. Use the ratting comb or knitting needle to make a straight part down the back. (It may tickle him!)

THE CASUAL TOPKNOT

The "official" show topknot is not for the faint of heart. It takes a lot of practice. Most people learn how to make this topknot from a mentor in the breed who has knowledge of grooming, exhibiting, and breeding. Demonstrating puppy and adult topknots for the show ring is beyond the scope of this book. The American Maltese Association website (americanmaltese.org) has a list of resources that cover advanced grooming.

Maltese are known for having topknot hairstyles.

For the everyday look, a nice single topknot looks adorable. Professional bows are available online, or you can find something cute at the pet boutique. Try to create a balanced look so that the bow(s) won't look out of place. Black bows look best, especially if your dog has good pigment. Reds and oranges can magnify the rust color of eye stains.

Start out by training your Maltese to lie with his head on a small pillow. The easiest way to do a topknot is simply to bundle the hair on top of the head with one or two latex bands, add a bow, and be done. Practice will make perfect.

HOW TO MAKE A TOPKNOT

For a polished single-topknot look:

1. Brush the hair back over the skull between the ears. The section of hair should be about 1 1/2 inches (4 cm) deep by 2 1/2 inches (6.5 cm) wide.
2. Using your parting comb, part the hair from the outside corner of one eye, then the other, and hold it up, making an inverted V.
3. Then part the hair again from one side to the other, creating a rectangle behind the inverted V.
4. If you wish, wrap a small piece of the home-perm endpaper or tissue around

the base of the hair to prevent damage.

5. Secure with the latex band, making sure the bands are not so tight that they cause the hair to pull around the eyes. Use the tip of the ratting comb to loosen the topknot a bit.
6. Make a nice poof on the underside of the band, leaving the hair loose on top of the band.
7. Attach your bow and admire your work.

It will take practice to get the topknot exactly right. You may even find your own way to do it.

DENTAL CARE

As your Maltese gets older, the number-one problem to avoid is periodontal disease, caused by an accumulation of plaque. Maltese have small, crowded mouths, making it easier for plaque to form. The first sign of plaque is usually bad breath, followed by gum swelling and soreness.

Plaque hardens into tartar, which cannot be removed by brushing and can lead to tooth loss if not treated. Eventually, bacteria from plaque and tartar can travel through the circulatory system and lodge in major organs, causing liver or kidney abscesses and damaging heart valves.

Brushing teeth is especially important for small breeds like the Maltese, who have crowded mouths that encourage plaque formation.

To prevent your Maltese from dental worries, brush your dog's teeth as often as possible, but at least once a week, with a soft-bristled toothbrush and canine toothpaste. Brush the inner surfaces as well as the outer, covering the crevices where the tooth and gum meet. Oral rinses formulated for use in pets can also be effective in plaque reduction.

This whole dental thing can be strange for some dogs. If you proceed too fast, your Maltese may become totally unwilling to let you try again. Short but fun training sessions usually create good results, and your pet will receive a lifetime of benefits. If a toothbrush doesn't work well for you, try dental pads, gauze, or sponges. They are not quite as effective but will help keep the teeth and gums clean.

CLEANING THE EARS

To get your Maltese accustomed to having his ears cleaned, handle and rub them gently during your usual cuddle sessions so that it won't be so traumatic when you begin to clean them.

The outer ear of the Maltese consists of the ear flap that funnels sound into the ear canal. Dogs have a long narrow ear canal that makes almost a 90-degree bend as it travels to the deeper parts of the ear, which is why it is so common for them to get ear infections. The ear flap contributes to the problem because it keeps the ear dark and moist. Signs of an ear infection are redness, discharge, odor, ear scratching, and head shaking.

If the inside of the ear has a lot of hair, that may increase the chance of an infection. To help prevent this:

1. Sprinkle the inside of the ear with antiseptic ear powder.

Handle and rub your Maltese's ears gently while cuddling so that ear cleaning will be more comfortable.

2. Give the powder a minute or two to numb the area, then pull a few hairs at a time.
3. Repeat until the hair is gone.

HOW TO CLEAN THE EARS

Use a good-quality liquid ear solution to clean the ears.

1. Pull back the ear flap to expose the inner side of the ear.
2. Instill the recommended number of drops into the ear canal, being careful not to touch the ear drum.
3. Massage the base of the ear to distribute the solution throughout the ear canal. Your Maltese will probably like this part.
4. Use cotton balls to remove debris from the inner side of the ear flap. Never use cotton-tip applicators in the ear canal.

Many people leave ear cleaning to a groomer or vet. If you see any signs of infection or ear mites (black, waxy discharge) or detect an unusual odor, your vet needs to see your Maltese as soon as possible for treatment.

CLEANING AROUND THE EYES

Certain lines of Maltese have a genetic predisposition to excessive tearing. Excess tearing onto the face creates a breeding ground for bacteria and yeast that causes the reddish-brown markings known as tearstains. Other factors that promote tearstains include health problems like ear infections and blocked tear ducts, cigarette smoke and other pollutants, and the ingestion of hard water, well water, and foods with red dye. Many breeders claim that stress can also cause staining due to excess tearing.

Puppies often have moderate to severe tearstaining when they cut their baby teeth and their permanent teeth. They also have to contend with puppy

Puppies usually outgrow tearstaining after they stop teething.

hair growing on the face, just long enough to poke the eyes and tear glands. Puppies usually outgrow the staining after they stop teething because tear production lessens.

HOW TO REMOVE TEARSTAINS

Removing tearstains can be tricky.

1. First you have to make sure the cause of the staining is gone. There are a few products on the market that work for nominal stains. For more severe stains, make a good paste of milk of magnesia, cornstarch, and peroxide (20 volume).
2. Carefully brush product into the stained area—not too close to the eye itself—and let dry overnight.
3. Wash out, and condition the hair well.
4. It may take several attempts for a badly stained face. Apply several days apart and keep the hair well-conditioned in between. Just be careful not to get product in your dog's eyes.

If all else fails, the hair will eventually grow out white once the cause of staining has been cleared up. While looking at the eyes, check to make sure they are not bloodshot, cloudy, or partially closed. If you find this, consult your vet at once.

For dogs genetically predisposed to staining, it may just take a little extra work to keep the area clean and dry. Keeping the eyes free of discharge will help prevent eye infections as well.

GENERAL EYE HEALTH

There are several other things you can do to keep your dog's eyes healthy, including using cornstarch or a baby washcloth to keep the area around the eyes dry and using your flea comb or cat comb to carefully remove any debris from the corner of the eye or the eyelashes. Always be careful with any grooming equipment around those big, beautiful eyes.

THE PEDICURE

Trimming a dog's nails is a tricky thing, but once you learn the basics, it can save you an outing. It *does* have to be done. If the nails become too long, they can actually interfere with your dog's walking. Untrimmed nails can split, resulting in pain and bleeding, or curl under and grow into the pad.

Nails usually need to be clipped monthly. Many dog owners choose to let their groomer or vet do it, and that is understandable. If you decide to give clipping a try, the first thing to do is very carefully trim the hair growing from the footpads so that it won't mat and cause pain when walking.

If you find a mat, separate the pads and trim it out with round-tipped scissors. Be careful! You don't want to nick the delicate skin between the pads.

Many dog owners let their groomer or veterinarian trim their dog's toenails.

Maltese tend to get agitated when you handle their front feet, so get your dog accustomed to having his feet handled while you are playing, if you can. It will make this task easier on both of you.

HOW TO CLIP YOUR MALTESE'S NAILS

Each nail has a blood vessel running through the center called the quick. The quick contains sensitive nerve endings that cause pain and bleeding when accidentally clipped. Therefore, the most important tool in clipping nails is your own sense of calm. If you trim the nail too closely, it may bleed, but one thing's for sure—your dog will yelp.

1. Start with your Maltese lying on his side, standing, or sitting in your lap. Whatever works. Hold his paw in one hand and the trimmer in the other.

2. Light-colored nails are easier to cut because you can see the blood vessels and nerves. Clip these nails within approximately 2 millimeters of the quick.

3. Clip dark-colored nails in very small increments to reduce the chance of cutting into the quick. As you clip deeper, you will see a gray-to-pink oval starting to appear at the top of the clipped surface of the nail. Stop clipping the nail at this point.

4. You can file the end of the nail to smooth the clipped surface.

I don't recommend nail grinders for a coated breed—it is so easy to catch errant hairs in the spinning part, and that will hurt your dog. The noise and vibration from these devices might be scary for your Maltese, too. Plus, they create dust that may get in his eyes—and yours.

Some Maltese have dewclaws, which are nails on the inside of the front legs (or, rarely, the back legs). Those nails have to be clipped as well or they will embed themselves into the dog's leg. Many breeders opt to have the dewclaws removed shortly after birth to prevent them from catching on things or ripping off in play.

HOW TO FIND A PROFESSIONAL GROOMER

As we have seen, you can do a lot of your dog's grooming yourself. Trimming your Maltese into a puppy clip is another matter. That typically takes a pro. But how can you find a good groomer?

First, ask your Maltese breeder for a recommendation if she lives in your area. She may even be a groomer herself. Friends and family or even your vet may have someone they know well from years of experience.

There are actually no requirements for a groomer to be licensed by a government agency, but many are certified or registered by organizations such as the National Dog Groomers Association of America (NDGAA). You can search for certified groomers near you on the NDGAA website, nationaldoggroomers.com.

Certification may not even be an issue. If a groomer is kind to your dog and presents your dog with a look that pleases you, that may be all you need. It is important that the dog looks forward to his grooming sessions and comes home happy.

CHOOSING YOUR GROOMER

Call ahead before meeting potential groomers and check their prices based on your breed and the condition your dog is in. Be honest if your Maltese is matted or dirty. This will take more of the groomer's time and increase the cost.

When you've found a potential match, take a tour of the establishment to make sure it is clean and the staff is friendly and courteous. Check doors and gates to make sure the facility is escape-proof. Since your Maltese will have to be dried, ask if they use a cage dryer, where the dog is actually in an enclosed cage. That method is too risky for a small dog like the Maltese. Ask them to use a stand-up or handheld blow dryer instead.

Let the groomer know of any medical issues your dog may have, such as diabetes, epilepsy, or arthritis. The salon will probably also ask for your dog's medical history and may require proof of vaccinations. They will want to know the name of your vet in case there is an emergency. This is for your dog's protection and that of the other dogs being groomed.

Ask the groomer if she ever uses sedation. This may not be acceptable to you, or you may want the sedative prescribed by your vet. And let her know if your dog is a biter. It is only fair to everyone.

Finally, do not be afraid to tell the groomer exactly what you want. If you don't want your Maltese trimmed like a Poodle, make that clear. Take along photos of cute puppy clips. Have realistic expectations, though. If your dog is matted, the groomer may not be able to save enough hair for the look you were hoping for. It may take a few trips to get your Maltese looking exactly like you want, but the effort will be worth it.

HEALTH OF YOUR MALTESE

The Maltese is a long-lived breed, with an average life span of 12 to 13 years or more. He is basically hearty and healthy. If you acquired your dog from a breeder who has kept accurate records, she will probably inform you of any possible medical disorders to be aware of. She knows her line of dogs better than anyone. Things *can* happen, just as with humans.

You, in cooperation with your veterinarian, are your dog's health care advocate. Your goal is to prevent health problems rather than have to deal with them. Just observe any physical changes in your Maltese and listen to him—he may be trying to tell you something.

FINDING A VETERINARIAN

The best way to find a good veterinarian is through referrals—from your Maltese breeder or from friends and relatives. If you can, stop by the clinic without your dog and make some observations.

- Is the facility clean and modern?
- Is the staff friendly to you and the clients in the waiting room?
- Is the waiting room overcrowded?
- Are the office hours convenient?
- Do they accept pet insurance?
- Do they have after-hours emergency coverage?

• Will you always see the same vet, or do they share clients?

If you are transferring from another clinic, be sure to have your records transferred before your first visit.

THE ANNUAL WELLNESS EXAM

The annual wellness exam is the first line of defense against many medical problems. Two blood tests, the complete blood count (CBC) and the chemistry panel, reveal diseases ranging from simple infections to liver or kidney problems, all things we would never detect otherwise. A blood test for heartworms should be done annually as well. Take a stool sample for your vet to check for parasites.

Your vet will also check for heart murmurs, lumps and bumps, and dental problems and take a look at the ears and eyes. Occasionally the exam will warrant further tests, and these tests could save your dog's life. The earlier any problem is discovered, the more likely it is to be treated and resolved.

Tell your vet about any subtle changes you have noticed in your Maltese. Has he been having accidents in the house? Is he drinking more water or not finishing his food? Has there been any discharge from his eyes or nose? Even seemingly insignificant behavior such as unusual stools, resisting exercise, or coughing could be significant. Don't be afraid to ask questions and take plenty of notes during the exam. And there is nothing wrong with asking for treatment costs and options. Vets are very good about factoring in finances.

If you are giving your Maltese any special diet, supplements, or holistic remedies, or any alternative medicine treatments, let your vet know. Also, if your dog has been seen by any other vets out of town or at the ER, take along those records.

VACCINATIONS

Vaccinations are undoubtedly one of the most significant advances in veterinary medicine. Cases of canine parvovirus and canine distemper have been greatly reduced, and one of the most feared diseases in history—rabies—has been virtually eradicated among our pet population.

Your vet knows your dog, his history, and what vaccines may be necessary for your unique locale. Let her know if your dog will be in contact with other dogs, such as in kennels, obedience classes, or dog parks, since these factors will impact your dog's risk of exposure to certain diseases. **Make sure that your vet is aware of any previous adverse reactions to vaccines.**

Very few dogs—less than one-half of one percent—have adverse reactions to vaccinations. Regardless, you should be aware of the most common reactions:

- Pain, swelling, or redness at the injection site or on the dog's face.
- A mild fever, decreased appetite, or depression.
- A mild cough from the intranasal bordetella and/or parainfluenza vaccine.
- Anaphylaxis, which may cause shock, respiratory failure, cardiac arrest, or death if not treated, usually occurs within minutes to hours. This is very rare—about one case in every 15,000 doses administered. If you observe diarrhea, vomiting, pale gums, cold limbs, fast heart rate, weak pulse, facial swelling, seizures, or shock, get emergency help immediately!

To be extra safe, make your appointment for vaccinations early in the morning so that you can watch your Maltese throughout the day while the clinic is still open. A puppy or dog whose immune system is compromised or stressed by illness or a surgical procedure should not be vaccinated. He may not be able to develop the necessary immunities.

VACCINE TITERS

If you have concerns about vaccinations, an antibody titer (blood test) can measure whether your Maltese is protected from a certain disease. Titers aren't yet available for all diseases and don't replace a vaccination program, but in some cases, they may help your vet determine if your dog really needs that vaccine.

During the annual wellness exam, your veterinarian will check your Maltese for general health and signs of illness.

CORE VACCINATIONS

Core vaccinations are for particularly dangerous diseases that are difficult to treat and easily transmitted. The American Animal Hospital Association (AAHA) recommends a series of core vaccinations during puppyhood and a booster one year later. These vaccinations, typically for distemper, adenovirus, and parvovirus, would then be administered every three years.

Distemper

Distemper is highly contagious and attacks the central nervous system. Signs include fever, discharge from the eyes and nose, loss of appetite, lethargy, seizures, and unique to distemper, hardening of the footpads and nose. Dogs can recover, but permanent brain damage can result. Treatment involves managing the signs until the virus has run its course.

Hepatitis

Caused by the canine adenovirus type 1 (CAV-1), hepatitis can produce death within hours and often affects young puppies most severely. Signs include fever, loss of appetite, runny nose and eyes, coughing, vomiting, jaundice, and swelling of the head, neck, and trunk. Sometimes you will see a bluish clouding of the cornea. Puppies who recover succumb more easily to kidney infections and may experience permanent liver damage and hampered eyesight. Your veterinarian will most likely manage symptoms until the virus runs its course.

Parvovirus

Parvovirus is spread through contact with infected feces and can live on inanimate surfaces. Dogs can be asymptomatic and still carry and shed the virus. There can be intestinal tract signs such as vomiting, putrid diarrhea, bloody feces, and in severe cases, fever, dehydration, and lowered white blood cell count. Or less commonly, it can manifest as a cardiac disease causing breathing difficulty and death in very young puppies (less than eight weeks of age). Older dogs who survive this form have scarring in the heart muscle. Treatment is managing the symptoms and secondary infections with fluids and antibiotics.

Rabies

Rabies is the only vaccination required by law, the frequency varying from state to state. The virus lives in the saliva of infected animals and is passed into the tissues of their bite victims. Rabies causes anxiety, partial paralysis, agitation, increase in saliva, difficulty swallowing, hydrophobia (fear of water), and ultimately death.

To reduce stress on your Maltese, arrange for him to receive the rabies vaccination separate from his other vaccinations. Also, never allow your Maltese to be vaccinated for any disease during a surgical procedure. That will put too much stress on his system.

NONCORE VACCINATIONS

Not all dogs should be vaccinated with all vaccines. For example, some areas may have a heavy incidence of Lyme disease, while others may have very few cases. Noncore vaccines should be given when the risk of the disease is significant in your geographical area or where you plan to travel. Your vet will consider your dog's risks in order to customize a vaccination program.

Bordetella (Kennel Cough)

Bordetella is a highly contagious respiratory disease characterized by inflammation of the trachea and bronchi. Signs include a dry, hacking cough that sounds like honking or retching and watery nasal discharge. In some cases, the dog may cough up white foam. In healthy adult dogs, this is a relatively minor

Dog Tale

Did you ever wonder why your injured Maltese suddenly seems okay once you get to the vet clinic, after you have called and begged for an emergency appointment? Stress causes a rise in cortisol, a hormone produced to manage stress, and endorphins, which interact with the brain to reduce our perception of pain. So don't feel bad if your Maltese is suddenly walking on that "injured" leg. Your description of his pain will help your vet make the diagnosis. It also doesn't hurt to have a video of the dog's behavior.

illness. However, in puppies or dogs in ill health, it can lead to pneumonia and death. Anti-inflammatory drugs help the coughing episodes, and antibiotics are used if pneumonia may be present. This vaccination is typically required within six months by boarding kennels and training classes, although an annual booster is considered adequate for protection.

Coronavirus

Coronavirus is an intestinal infection that usually produces a mild disease but can be severe in young puppies. Early signs are depression with loss of appetite, followed by vomiting and the passage of a foul-smelling, yellow-to-orange diarrhea. Treatment includes keeping the dog hydrated and controlling vomiting and diarrhea. The American Veterinary Medical Association (AVMA) does not recommend this vaccine because the disease responds readily to treatment and the vaccine may cause an adverse reaction.

Leptospirosis

Leptospirosis is caused by *Leptospira* bacteria, which are spread in urine. Most infections are mild and can include fever, loss of appetite, vomiting, lethargy, and sometimes diarrhea or blood in the urine. Following recovery, untreated dogs can become carriers and shed bacteria in their urine for up to a year. Blood tests confirm the diagnosis. Antibiotics are effective, as are supportive measures. Humans can get leptospirosis, so precautions should be taken if the family dog has it. This vaccine has been associated with severe reactions and death more than other vaccines, so discuss this thoroughly with your vet.

PARASITES

A parasite is an organism that inhabits and finds nourishment from another creature. In exchange for our dogs providing this warm, cozy place to live, the parasites reproduce rapidly and reward their hosts with illness and even death.

Be sure to take along a stool sample, which can be checked for internal parasites, when your Maltese goes in for his exam. This way the vet will not have to extract a sample, which would be very uncomfortable for your dog!

EXTERNAL PARASITES

Ear Mites

Ear mites are arachnids that can make your Maltese miserable if they decide to reside in his ear canal. They can cause itching, and if left untreated, hearing loss.

The dog's incessant scratching can set the stage for secondary bacterial or fungal infections. Mites leave a trail of dark reddish-brown, crumbly debris. Your vet will probably clean the ears for you and prescribe a topical medication and ear wash.

Your veterinarian may prescribe ear wash and other medications if your Maltese has ear mites.

Fleas

Fleas are the bane of a dog's existence. Not only are they annoying to the dog, but they can cause flea-allergy dermatitis, and in very small dogs like the Maltese, they can even cause anemia from ingesting too much blood. Some carry tapeworms and various blood-borne infections.

With fleas, prevention is the best medicine. Ask your vet about topical or oral flea preventives that contain repellents, insecticides, or IGRs and interrupt the flea's life cycle. Flea products generally are safe, but toxicity can occur if the dog gets an overly large dosage. Dogs under 20 pounds (9 kg) have the greatest chance of having a reaction. Just be careful with your little guy and don't assume more is better!

Ringworm

Ringworm, a fungal infection that invades the hair and hair follicles, is primarily a disease of puppies and young adults. Typical areas of involvement are the face, ears, paws, and tail. Found on carpets, brushes, combs, toys, and furniture, ringworm is transmitted by spores in the soil and by contact with the infected hair of dogs and cats. Humans can get ringworm from their pets and vice versa.

Ringworm gets its name from its appearance as a spreading circle of hair loss and scaly skin. It is usually not itchy, but a secondary bacterial infection can cause itchiness. The treatment is a topical antifungal agent containing miconazole and antifungal shampoo.

Ticks

Ticks are arachnids that bite and fasten themselves onto the skin and feed on blood. Wild ticks live in the feathers and fur of many birds and animals. Deer ticks, which carry Lyme disease, like shaded sites in the woods or in home landscapes—wherever deer like to go.

Most ticks do not carry disease, but it's important to remove a tick as soon as you find it, as they must be attached for 24 to 36 hours to transfer pathogens to you or your Maltese. Removing the tick also helps you prevent a skin infection. Tick-transmitted diseases include Lyme disease, Rocky Mountain spotted fever, anemia, and tick-bite paralysis.

INTERNAL PARASITES

Heartworms

Heartworms are by far the most dangerous parasites, and the treatment is the most extensive and costly. Fortunately, they are also the easiest parasites to guard against.

Check your Maltese for ticks whenever he plays in wilderness areas.

Heartworms are spread by mosquitoes and live in the right side of the heart. Recently infected dogs may show no signs of the disease, while heavily infected dogs may eventually show a mild, persistent cough, reluctance to exercise, fatigue, reduced appetite, and weight loss. Some will accumulate fluid in the abdomen, making them look pot-bellied.

The best way to prevent a heartworm infection is to give your Maltese preventive medications such as monthly tablets or chewables. These medications interrupt heartworm development before adult worms reach the lungs and cause disease. Some topical heartworm preventives even control other parasites, such as fleas and other worms.

Hookworms

Hookworms attach themselves to the lining of the intestinal tract and feed on the dog's blood. Infection is often passed from a mother to her puppies, but adults can get them from infested soil or raw food. The dog may have diarrhea that is black and tarry from digested blood. Hookworms can be rapidly lethal to puppies.

Roundworms

Roundworms are spaghetti-like in shape and can grow to 4 or 5 inches (10 or 12.5 cm) in the dog's small intestine. The female worms produce eggs that are passed in the stool where they may be inadvertently ingested by other dogs. Often there are no clinical signs, but puppies show vomiting, diarrhea, and a pot-bellied appearance.

Tapeworms

Tapeworms are segmented parasites that embed themselves inside a dog's small intestine. Segments containing egg packets break off the worm's body and are deposited outside with the feces, or you may find them stuck on your dog's behind. They actually look like grains of rice. This will probably cause your Maltese to scoot his behind on the carpet because the pieces will be irritating. Dogs can become infected by eating fleas that contain immature tapeworms. Sometimes your dog may show no signs, but vomiting and diarrhea can develop. Tapeworms are killed by a medication called *praziquantel*.

Whipworms

Whipworms are normally found in the lower intestine and can cause acute inflammation, difficult bowel movements, anemia, and weight loss. Infections are comparatively resistant to medication. It may take several months to rid your environment, especially soil, of both adult and larval whipworms.

SPAYING/NEUTERING YOUR MALTESE

Spaying and neutering are surgical procedures performed by a veterinarian, for female and male dogs respectively, that render dogs incapable of reproducing.

This is a hot topic in veterinary medicine. Some studies show long-term side effects from early spaying and neutering, while others support the current procedures. Talk to your vet and your dog's breeder about how this controversy affects your Maltese.

YOUR FEMALE MALTESE

If your female Maltese is spayed before her first heat cycle, she will most likely never develop a mammary tumor. When spayed after one heat cycle, her risk of developing a mammary tumor grows slightly, and her chances increase to 25 percent after more than one cycle. Some breeders feel spaying before the first heat cycle (at approximately five months old) is too young for a toy breed such as the Maltese. They may suggest you wait until the 9-to-12-month range.

Without spaying, females may endure: false pregnancies, which are sad to watch and can lead to mastitis (because of retained milk in the mammary glands); staining, odor, and urine marking during heat cycles; a life-threatening infection called pyometra (literally, pus in the uterus); and unplanned pregnancy.

Females occasionally develop urinary tract problems due to a drop in estrogen levels after being spayed. This also happens to seniors. It begins with a strong urine odor; then the dog dribbles. Fortunately, this is an easy condition to treat with medication, and there is a surgical procedure where the bladder is actually repositioned to reduce dribbling.

YOUR MALE MALTESE

Neutering the male is low-risk and relatively inexpensive, especially for such a small dog. There is some debate as to how early dogs can be neutered, but most are neutered between five and eight months of age, before unwanted behaviors have started. Maltese usually start becoming sexually mature after nine months of age, so prior to that may be the best time for your male to be neutered.

The benefits of neutering your male are preventing the more pungent odor of urine; reducing the occurrence of abscesses, cysts, and prostatic hyperplasia (and of perineal hernias in older males); and lowering the likelihood of behavioral issues, including housetraining difficulties, roaming, and territory marking. If your Maltese is a monorchid—that is, has one retained testicle—it is even more important to neuter him. If you don't, he will be much more likely to develop cancer in the retained testicle.

On the other hand, studies have shown that neutered males are at significantly higher risk for developing prostate, bladder, and other forms of cancer. There may also be a risk of skeletal problems and joint disease among early-neutered dogs. This research is evolving, so it is best to make the decision with your dog's breeder and your vet based on what is best for your boy.

BREED-SPECIFIC HEALTH CONCERNS

The majority of Maltese go through life without encountering any of the following medical issues, but as a Maltese owner, it is best to be aware of them just in case. For more information about these medical issues and to keep up with new findings, visit the American Maltese Association's health information resources at americanmaltese.org.

COLLAPSED TRACHEA

The trachea (or "windpipe") is held open by rings of cartilage. If that cartilage weakens, the trachea may begin to collapse, and the amount of air able to get through is severely restricted, putting excess stress on the heart and lungs. This problem can be made worse by heat, humidity, and excitement. Small-breed dogs are more likely to be affected by this condition, particularly as they age. The most common sign is a chronic, nonproductive, honking cough, sometimes accompanied by vomiting.

Diagnosis is made by X-rays or endoscopy. Medication may control the cough and inflammation and open up the airway. Isolate your dog from irritants such as cigarette smoke, noxious fumes, or excessive dust. Make sure he is not overweight and restrict his exercise. To protect his throat and keep pressure off the airway,

Small dogs are more likely to experince collapsed trachea.

use a harness rather than a collar on your walks. If the signs become severe, surgery may be in order.

CONGESTIVE HEART FAILURE (CHF)

Dogs don't have heart attacks, per se. Most canine heart disorders will likely progress to congestive heart failure (CHF) if not recognized early. With CHF, the heart becomes gradually unable to pump blood efficiently and becomes overly filled with blood. Excess fluid accumulates in the lungs or within the chest, abdomen, and other body cavities. Without intervention, the dog is likely to die soon afterward. With the proper treatment, including diuretics and drugs, a dog may survive for months and even years.

Be aware of any coughing, resistance to exercise, and refusal to eat. Because excess fat around the heart and blood vessels can reduce your dog's chance of survival, weight control and exercise are very important.

DENTAL ISSUES

Maltese are prone to tarter buildup, gingivitis, early tooth loss, and plaque formation because of their small, sometimes crowded mouths. If gums become sore or teeth become infected, bacteria can actually travel to various parts of the body via the circulatory system and lodge in major organs, causing microscopic lesions. Then the bacteria can damage delicate heart valves or cause liver or kidney abscesses.

With the breed's predisposition to heart disease, this must be avoided, and it can. Regular dental care as described in the chapter on grooming can help prevent these serious systemic problems.

EYE DISORDERS

One of the most endearing characteristics of the Maltese is those big dark eyes staring up at you. You want to keep them healthy. There are several eye disorders you should be on the lookout for, most of which can be treated early and easily to prevent complications.

- **Distichiasis** is when small eyelashes grow on the inner surface or very edge of the eyelids, irritating the cornea, making the eye red and inflamed and possibly causing discharge. In severe cases, the cornea may become ulcerated and blindness can result. The abnormal eyelashes should be removed surgically. This is considered an inherited disease.
- **Entropion** is an inward rolling of the eyelid edges, causing the hair on the affected lid to continuously rub against the cornea. This can cause significant discomfort and trauma to the cornea. Surgical correction is necessary.

PUPPY POINTER

Young Maltese puppies are susceptible to hypoglycemia (low blood sugar). A lot of events can act as triggers, including stress, missing a meal, overplaying, vaccinations, intestinal parasites, and chronic illness. So-called "teacup" Maltese are particularly prone to hypoglycemia. Signs may include weakness, confusion, wobbly gait, and seizures. If not remedied, the puppy could have convulsions, go into shock, and possibly become comatose. If you suspect an episode of hypoglycemia, immediately give him some corn syrup, honey, or table sugar. Rub it on his gums if he cannot swallow. Then take him immediately to your vet. If your dog is hypoglycemic, give him frequent small meals and talk to your vet about prevention and treatment options. The outlook is very good; he will likely outgrow it.

- **Keratoconjunctivitis sicca (dry eye syndrome)** is caused by inadequate tear production. Signs are thick, yellow discharge, redness, and rubbing at the eyes. Eye drops are prescribed to stimulate tear production, decrease scar tissue, and prevent corneal ulcers and vision loss.

HEART MURMURS

Heart murmurs are graded on a scale of one to six, with grade six being the loudest and most severe. The most common causes of heart murmurs in Maltese are mitral valve dysplasia (MVD) and patent ductus arteriosus (PDA).

Sometimes puppies will have a mild (grade one or two) murmur, called an "innocent" or "flow" murmur, which they outgrow as they mature. But if a puppy has a grade three or higher murmur or any murmur that persists past 16 weeks of age, there is a significant concern for a congenital heart abnormality.

Many older dogs with serious heart murmurs appear to have no sign of slowing down, which is great, but this is yet another reason why annual exams are necessary.

HEPATIC MICROVASCULAR DYSPLASIA

When certain microscopic blood vessels in the liver are underdeveloped or absent, the liver becomes small (atrophied) and the dog can no longer process toxins or make proteins necessary for growth. This is called hepatic microvascular dysplasia (HMD or MVD). Maltese with HMD can have the same clinical signs as those with a portosystemic shunt (PSS), listed below, or have no signs at all. A definitive diagnosis is made by ruling out PSS.

There is no surgical treatment for HMD. Dogs with the condition are managed medically, and treatment is based on the severity of the condition. As with PSS, veterinary diets are used along with lactulose and other supplements. Most dogs with HMD do well on diet change alone.

MALTESE ENCEPHALITIS

Maltese encephalitis is a term that encompasses several inflammatory diseases of the central nervous system, including granulomatous meningoencephalomyelitis (GME) and necrotizing meningoencephalitis (NME). Maltese appear to be prone to the more deadly form, NME, which causes inflammation of the brain and cell death.

Neurological encephalitis signs depend on what area or areas of the central nervous system are involved. Affected dogs can develop seizures, depression, difficulty walking, circling, and blindness. Survival ranges from several days to three to six months. An MRI and cerebrospinal fluid (CSF) analysis are helpful in diagnosing this disorder, but there is no way to confirm a diagnosis except to evaluate the brain tissue after the dog has died. Aggressive early treatment with steroids and chemotherapy treatment can put a dog into remission. There may be a genetic test for this tragic disorder very soon.

MITRAL VALVE DYSPLASIA (MVD)

A 2011 study by the University of Georgia College of Veterinary Medicine reported that 21 percent of Maltese deaths are related to cardiovascular disease, which is compatible with the incidence of mitral valve disease in the breed.

The mitral valve is a one-way valve in the left side of the heart, between the upper chamber (atrium) and lower chamber (ventricle). Normally, blood only goes from the atrium to the ventricle. However, in some dogs, this one-way valve starts to leak. Blood squirts backward up through the valve into the atrium, causing turbulence. The extra blood flow stretches out the atrium

Dogs with mitral valve dysplasia (MVD) should avoid strenuous exercise, extreme humidity, and high temperatures.

over time, pulling the valve open even farther, meaning even more blood can leak. This condition is called mitral valve dysplasia (MVD).

A dog who is mildly affected may live many years, while a severely affected dog may survive only a few months after diagnosis. Dogs with MVD should avoid strenuous exercise, extreme humidity, and high temperatures. The only cure for MVD is valve replacement surgery, which is not widely available. MVD can be treated with diuretics to help make the dog more comfortable if breathing becomes labored.

PATELLAR LUXATION

Many small breeds are prone to patellar luxation, which is basically a loose or displaced patella (kneecap). The ridges forming the patellar groove are too shallow, causing the patella to jump out of the groove sideways. You may notice mild to moderate lameness, or you may see your Maltese stretch his leg backward in an effort to reduce the pain. Patellar luxation may be congenital or caused by trauma.

Patellar luxation has been graded on a scale of zero to four based on how easily the kneecap can be manipulated in and out of its groove on orthopedic examination. Surgical treatment is typically considered in grades two and over. Slippery floors can sometimes be difficult to maneuver for a dog with patellar luxation, so make sure he has stable footing and a bed he can easily get into. You can help prevent a knee injury by keeping your Maltese from jumping.

PORTOSYSTEMIC SHUNT (PSS)

Small breeds are prone to portosystemic shunts (PSS), or "liver shunts." One of the liver's main functions is detoxifying substances as they pass through the bloodstream. When a dog has PSS, blood flow bypasses the liver and brings toxic matter through the rest of the circulatory system. Signs include ataxia (swaying as if intoxicated), seizures, blindness, and head pressing.

Management of PSS consists of a low-protein diet. The condition can also be treated with prescription and nonprescription medications, but surgery is often necessary to narrow or tie off the abnormal shunt vessel. Despite these treatment options, liver shunts are often fatal.

REVERSE SNEEZE (INSPIRATORY PAROXYSMAL RESPIRATION)

The reverse sneeze can be terrifying the first time you hear it. Your dog will make a loud snorting sound as he attempts to clear his nose and throat by

Reverse sneezing stops on its own, but you can massage your Maltese's throat to help the sneezing pass.

inhaling a sneeze rather than exhaling. This display is caused by allergies, dust, cigarette smoke, or a bit of mucus—anything that causes a normal sneeze. Dogs lower to the ground like the Maltese are more prone to the reverse sneeze, but it can occur in any breed.

You don't really have to do anything when it happens because it will stop on its own. It is very hard to stand by and watch, though. Here are a few things you can try:

- Take his mind off the attack by placing your finger on his tongue or over his nose.
- Massage his throat from the jaw to the larynx.
- Put your fingers over his nostrils to force him to breathe through his mouth, massaging his throat if possible.

If your Maltese reverse sneezes too often, check with your vet to rule out canine nasal mites, polyps, or an upper respiratory condition.

WHITE SHAKER DOG SYNDROME

This disorder primarily affects white dogs, such as Maltese, West Highland White Terriers, and Samoyeds. It causes a diffuse tremor over the entire body.

Other signs are lack of coordination, head tilt, and rapid eye movement. The dog remains alert during these episodes. The condition usually manifests when the dog is six months to three years old and becomes stressed or overly excited. It isn't painful and doesn't affect the dog's personality.

Most dogs recover completely with early treatment with corticosteroids and possibly diazepam (Valium). Signs usually begin to improve within a few days. The cause is unknown, although it may be a disease of the immune system or result from an inflammation or infection of the brain.

ALTERNATIVE THERAPIES

Many of us have turned to various forms of alternative therapies or medicines for our own ailments, either exclusively or in conjunction with traditional Western medicine. Fortunately, there are alternative treatments available for your Maltese as well.

ACUPUNCTURE

Acupuncture has been practiced for nearly 4,000 years in traditional Chinese medicine. Using fine needles, it stimulates specific body points aligned with the central nervous system and various organs. It is used to treat a range of conditions from joint disease to allergies and has made a big difference in returning mobility to dogs with arthritis. Acupuncture is even used for behavioral problems like separation anxiety and thunderstorm phobia. Acupressure works in the same way but manually applies pressure to stimulate key points.

CHIROPRACTIC

Chiropractic, just as in human medicine, works for patients who have problems with the spine, bones, joints, or muscles by employing manual manipulation of the spine. The primary national credential for this field in North America is from the American Veterinary Chiropractic Association (AVCA).

HERBAL

Herbal medicine has been around for millennia and was most likely used to treat ancient Maltese dogs as well as their humans. The use of herbs and their derivatives as therapeutic agents include treatments for anxiety, urinary tract infections, gastrointestinal problems, motion sickness, and reproductive disorders. Please don't try herbal remedies on your Maltese without qualified guidance.

Herbal medicine has been around for millennia and was most likely used to treat ancient Maltese dogs as well as their humans.

HOLISTIC

Holistic veterinarians review each dog's behavioral patterns, dietary and medical history, and emotional environment. They then create treatment regimens drawing from therapies such as acupuncture, chiropractic, herbs, massage, nutrition, and others, including traditional medicines.

FIRST AID

Dogs can be dogs. Just like human kids, they can injure themselves playing. Having a canine first-aid kit on hand will reduce the stress of a mishap. Some obvious items to have on hand are bandages, adhesive tape, cotton swabs, and a wound disinfectant. Have your veterinarian's number on speed dial or on your smartphone. Another number is the ASPCA Animal Poison Control Center at (888) 426-4435. There may be a fee for this call, but the call could save your dog's life.

SENIOR DOGS

A mistake many of us make with our senior dogs is that we assume something we observe is "just due to old age." Old age is not a disease; it is just a life stage. With all the advances in senior dog health care over the years, there is an even greater opportunity for us to give our Maltese a long, quality life.

A dog is considered to be a senior when he has passed through the age calculated to represent 75 percent of his anticipated life span. A 10-year-old Maltese might be the equivalent of a 56-year-old man. At age 14, he is the equivalent of a 72-year-old.

Schedule a semi-annual wellness checkup for your senior that includes an extensive physical exam and blood work. Tell your vet about any changes you have noticed. They may be a warning sign of something that can be remedied. Conditions to watch out for in your senior Maltese include canine cognitive dysfunction (CCD), which causes signs such as confusion and disorientation, barking for no reason, and house soiling; intervertebral disk disease, which hampers movement in the spine; and osteoarthritis, which makes movement painful and affects overweight dogs more acutely.

TRAINING YOUR MALTESE

Maltese are so toylike, so small and adorable, that sometimes we don't realize they need the same training and guidance a large dog needs. By developing a strong bond with you through training, your dog will learn what is expected of him, whether it is basic math or how to sit and stay. This will reduce frustration for both of you.

WHY TRAIN YOUR DOG?

A dog as portable as a Maltese can be carried with you anywhere dogs are allowed—and a well-trained dog is more likely to be included when you are a guest in another home. Basic obedience commands such as *sit* and *stay* will also make a medical exam or a toenail clipping a lot easier. That is not to say that he will necessarily stand still the first few times—or ever—but it is a goal you can strive for. Plus, a well-trained dog will be less of a risk of biting someone.

Whether a puppy or an adult, your dog needs to learn the rules of the household from the start. Which toys are his and which ones belong to his humans? Which pieces of furniture can he snooze on, if any? And most importantly, where does he go to the bathroom? Everyone in the household needs to learn the rules and help the new family member adapt by applying them with consistency. Just be firm and don't let him outsmart you with that endearingly sweet face. A well-behaved Maltese is so much easier to live with than one who is spoiled!

POSITIVE TRAINING

For many years, trainers used harsh methods and negative reinforcement to train dogs, with the understanding that the dog does what you want in order to escape an unpleasant experience, even punishment. Even at its best, dog training consisted of repetitive on-leash obedience drills. Fortunately, in the past few decades, positive reinforcement methods have been adapted by most trainers and are now the norm.

Positive training works because no force, pain, or intimidation is used. Instead, the dog learns the behaviors with good associations attached. This is known as operant conditioning. Basically, we reward desired behavior and ignore unwanted behavior. These positive responses to undesirable behavior, combined with basic training, keep the dog from forming negative associations with people. As your dog learns to look to you for leadership, the bond between you will strengthen.

The highly popular clicker-training method uses a small plastic device that makes a short, distinct "click" sound. This click tells the dog exactly when he has performed a behavior that will earn him a reward. Combined with a training command, a treat, and other positive reinforcement, this is an effective, humane way to teach any animal any behavior he is capable of doing.

Using positive training methods does not mean that your dog will never have to be corrected. For example, you might take away what your dog was playing with when he was bad. Or if he misbehaved while you were at the cookie jar, no cookie. Gentle verbal reprimands and time-outs are fine as well. Another tried-and-true method is to ignore your Maltese when he is being naughty. Dogs tend to do what benefits them at the moment. If whining, for example, causes your dog to get zero attention, sometimes he will stop the behavior.

Maltese are highly intelligent, enthusiastic dogs. Using positive reinforcement, you can reward him for doing things you want him to do. You can use treats, toys, physical affection, verbal praise, or all of the above to reward your dog for correct behavior.

SOCIALIZATION

Socialization means exposing your Maltese to different environments, teaching him to interact acceptably with humans and other animals, and providing the opportunity for a little exploration. Puppies are capable of learning at an incredibly quick pace, so you should expose him to as many (safe) stimuli as

Socializing your Maltese involves teaching him to interact acceptably with humans and other animals.

possible, just as you would a human child. This will help your puppy grow up to be a friendly, confident, reliable, and happy member of your family.

When you bring your Maltese home, make sure he has pottied outdoors (with lots of praise), then let him inside so that he can quietly explore his new house. He needs to learn gradually about his new domain—vacuum cleaners, doorbells, different floor surfaces, cars racing by, and children playing in the neighborhood. Make sure all experiences are safe and positive for your puppy. If he cringes from a noise, divert his attention to something more pleasant. Don't soothe or baby him too much—he may become too dependent on you. You will eventually discover the best way to console him, so just do your best and enjoy these delightful moments of puppyhood.

Ideally, your Maltese should meet all kinds of people—children, the elderly, people who use canes, men with beards, etc. Ask your guests to sit on the floor if they can and let your puppy go to them. He will probably want to sniff their hands and maybe even do a little dance to show off. Encourage good behavior with praise or a treat. This is his time to shine—to bask in all the attention. He should thoroughly enjoy this playtime.

Your Maltese will have fun visiting the local dog park or going for a walk to size up the neighborhood. Many dog parks have special areas for small dogs. You may even find local classes or playgroups for puppies, which will allow him to play and learn with dogs his own age and size. Before you enroll in classes, however, find out what training methods are used so that your puppy will not be exposed to harsh situations. And a word of caution about dog parks and other public places. Not all dogs are well-behaved, even if they appear to be when you first meet them. Maltese are very small dogs and might feel the need to defend their honor!

CRATE TRAINING

Crates get a bad rap, but they aren't "dog jails" unless you make them so. Dogs, even that silky-haired, wide-eyed treasure of yours, are den animals. They crave the comfort of small, confined spaces.

Until your puppy is allowed to run free, staying in a crate keeps him from nibbling on a prized possession or a dangerous electrical cord, getting into the trash, or running unnoticed into a forbidden room. A crate is a very effective way to housetrain your Maltese, and if used correctly, it will become his private den. If he travels in the car or stays with you in a motel on vacation, the crate will become familiar territory for an unfamiliar circumstance.

Throughout the life of your Maltese, a crate in your home can be a lifesaver. He can stay there, securely, if workers are in the house, if you have company who are not fond of dogs (yes, there are such people!), or if you are expecting a delivery and don't want him running for the door.

HIS NEW ABODE

It is easy to understand why your Maltese may be resistant to getting inside the crate. He has left the warmth of his mother and littermates, followed by the attention and cuddles from his new family. He may want to hang out with you rather than taking on this new behavior. However, learning to stay inside the crate is a must for him to become a well-mannered, housetrained pet.

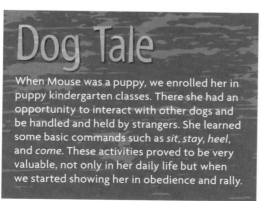

Dog Tale

When Mouse was a puppy, we enrolled her in puppy kindergarten classes. There she had an opportunity to interact with other dogs and be handled and held by strangers. She learned some basic commands such as *sit, stay, heel*, and *come*. These activities proved to be very valuable, not only in her daily life but when we started showing her in obedience and rally.

CRATE LOCATION

Choose a place for the crate where your Maltese will be

among his family. Make sure it is away from drafts or heat registers. Attach a water bottle to the inside of the crate or use a small water bowl that attaches on the inside. Maltese are too small to go without water for long. You may want to feed his meals inside the crate.

CRATE SIZE

As for the size of the crate, choose one large enough for your Maltese to comfortably lie down, stand up, and turn around in. If the crate is too large, he might soil one end of it and sleep at the other. You can buy crates with dividers to make the area smaller at first; then you can take out the divider as the little guy grows.

BE AWARE!

Make sure that your Maltese has the appropriate vaccinations, as well as flea and heartworm preventives, before taking him to a dog park or training class. And for your dog's safety, don't let him interact with another dog until you get to know him, especially if the other dog is much larger. Your Maltese doesn't know how small he is!

Buy one portable enough to carry into the bedroom at night so that you can hear whining, circling, barking, or scratching to go outside. Since Maltese have very small feet, avoid crates with grates or wire flooring, which can catch their feet and toes and cause serious injury.

HOW TO CRATE TRAIN

Sometimes it helps to start crate training when your Maltese is tired from playing and wants to take a snooze. Leave the crate door open. When he walks in, if he seems content, let him be for a while. If he seems hesitant, encourage and praise him. Most dogs will become enticed by the open door and see the crate as an escape from their humans. They find the same comfort and solace in their crates as their ancestors found in their dens.

Praise him any time he goes in so that he will know this is one great place to be. You can give him a command such as "bed." When he goes inside the crate and you close the door, say, "Bed!" and keep praising him, gradually increasing the time the door is closed. Eventually, he will associate the command word with going to his crate and will go in on command.

For safety's sake, take his collar off before putting him in the crate if there is anything for the collar to catch on. Collars can get caught, causing your dog to panic, and an injury could occur.

HOUSETRAINING

As soon as a newborn puppy can crawl, he will manage to get out of his sleeping area to relieve himself. This is why crate training works—the puppy learns that when the urge to urinate or defecate occurs, he can "hold it" to avoid soiling his space. You will want to take advantage of this instinct and teach your puppy or new adult basic potty manners.

HOW TO HOUSETRAIN

The key to successful housetraining is anticipating when your dog needs to go. By taking him outside at that point, you're giving him a chance to succeed. If he has been crated overnight or for a few hours during the day, he will probably be anxious to get out and go to his designated area. The movement of running will make him want to go even more. At the door, ask, "Outside?" Then as you go out, repeat. Watch him to make sure that he takes care of business.

You may want to train him to go to a certain part of the yard for convenience of cleaning up. Be sure to reward him for going in the right place. Once he has been good, praise him and let him run and play. Watch for cues that he has to "go" while he is playing, such as circling or sniffing the ground. If he whines while crated, this may also be a sign.

It is difficult to say how often your little Maltese will have to go out. There is a fine line between taking him out too often, so that he loses sight of why he is going out in the first place, and not taking him out enough and chancing an accident. Try a schedule that suits your family's activities, such as first thing in the morning, at lunchtime when you might be coming home to let him out, at dinnertime, and again at bedtime. You may have to set your alarm and take him out a few times during the night at first. And don't forget to take him out after he has eaten and after he has played.

The key to successful housetraining is anticipating when your dog needs to go.

Resist the urge to carry your Maltese outside. Encourage him to walk on his own, as he will have to do as an adult. He needs to learn the route on his own—the smells, the sights and sounds. And always use the same door, always walk to the same spot, and always give the same command.

Keep in mind that a Maltese has a smaller bladder than

PUPPY POINTER

Maltese are very bright, so you have to be consistent. If you feed your dog once from the table, he will expect it in the future. If you let him play on the bed, he will think it is *his* bed. Decide what kind of adult you want him to be and apply the rules early.

a larger dog does, so allow at least several months for him to become trained. However, he might surprise you and take to it very quickly! Crate training, if done properly, will give your Maltese no opportunity for error.

ACCIDENTS

If you catch your puppy having an accident, don't punish him! Interrupt him by gently telling him, "No," and take him outside. When he goes in the proper place, praise him enthusiastically or give him a treat. If he has an accident but you don't catch him, don't yell or punish him. Clean it up with a good enzyme cleaner and forget it. He will have no idea what the scolding is for. He doesn't have the capacity to put the punishment together with something he has done more than a few minutes ago.

If you can't come home during your work day, consider having someone stop by to let him out. The more times he soils the crate, the more likely he is to think that this behavior is all right after all.

INDOOR TRAINING

Some Maltese caregivers opt to use indoor piddle pads. In some cases, such as apartment living, this may be necessary, and with travel it can be a real convenience. Piddle pads have a non-skid plastic backing, absorbent layers, and leak-proof edges. You can buy a plastic tray to anchor the pad in or use a cat litter box. Newspapers are not a good choice for a white dog, as the ink will rub off on his coat and make a mess.

Training your puppy to use piddle pads is similar to training him to go outside— you just put him on the pad instead of taking him out. Put him on the pad first thing in the morning and any other time he has been crated. However, if you can avoid indoor training, do so, because once the behavior goes on for a long time it may be difficult to change. Outdoor potty training tends to make more sense to your dog because of the obvious difference from indoors. With indoor potty training, you're teaching him to go in the house, so the distinctions aren't as clear. Also note that indoor training is no substitute for taking your dog for a nice walk!

BASIC COMMANDS

Let's face it. For thousands of years, Maltese have had it made. Unlike their relatives, they did not have to hunt, herd, or guard. Other than the occasional request to serve as foot warmers or heating pads for their humans, they have lived a very cushy life.

Genetically, however, they are dogs. They communicate by using looks, posture, smells, and sounds. Theoretically they are reliable and predictable, but if you have lived with a Maltese, you know that isn't necessarily true. They can be ornery little beings and have minds of their own!

The key issue with positive-reinforcement dog training is consistency. The more consistent you are with your commands, the more reliable your Maltese will be in responding. And whether you use food or praise as a reward, or use the clicker method, feeling comfortable with the method is what is really important.

Once your Maltese has a feel for listening to you and working with you, start with some basic commands.

GETTING STARTED

Once your Maltese has a feel for listening to you and working with you, start with some basic commands. Small pieces of cheese, hot dog, dried liver, or whatever he likes can be used to entice him to learn. You can buy small bags to attach to your belt to make it easier to reach the treat. If you prefer to reward your Maltese with praise, this works very well, too. Some dogs are just as happy with that extra-special attention.

Training a dog as small as a Maltese has its challenges. As comfortable as he may be with you, he is still arching his neck back to look at you—you are very tall to him! One option for beginning training is to sit on the floor with your dog on your left side to teach the commands.

There are four obedience commands that can literally save your dog's life, not to mention help make your Maltese a suitable host when you have company: *down*, *stay*, and *come*. Two others, *sit* and *heel*, are important in a lot of situations, including going for a walk.

Always train with your Maltese secure on his leash or in a fenced-in area when not training inside. And vary the locations so that he will find new distractions in other environments. All of the commands mentioned below can, and should, be preceded by your dog's name in order to get his attention.

The *sit* command is useful for keeping your Maltese from wandering away.

THE *SIT* COMMAND

The *sit* command is useful for keeping your dog at your side rather than him jumping up on a visitor or trying to wander off.

How to Teach *Sit*

You can start training your dog to sit when he sits on his own. When you see him sit, say, "Sit!" immediately and praise and give him a treat. See how you can make him think this was all his idea? Eventually he should sit for longer periods of time.

If you are unable to capture that moment when your Maltese sits, try this:

1. With a treat in your hand, hold it above his head (but not so high that he'll want to jump for it) and move it back. This should automatically cause him to sit.
2. Say, "Sit!" and give him the treat only if he's still in the sitting position.
3. If he gets up, try again.
4. Start with 15 seconds before giving him the treat, and then 30 seconds, working your way to one minute.

THE *DOWN* COMMAND

The *down* command can be a lifesaver if your Maltese should escape from the yard or get loose from his leash. If you see him nearing a busy street or other danger, you can yell, "Down!" and he will go down and stay until you can put his collar back on or pick him up. After your heart stops frantically beating, be sure to praise him for a job well done. (Don't punish him for escaping. It will be the *down* that he will associate with the praise.)

The *down* can also be used to ensure that your Maltese is safely in place if, for example, a door opens unexpectedly and you are unable to pick him up in time.

How to Teach *Down*

As with the *sit* command, the easiest way to teach *down* is by taking the opportunity to say "Down!" precisely when he lies down on his own. Then praise and reward him. If you can't catch him in a *down*, you may have to entice him with a treat.

1. Lower the treat to the ground in front of his paws to help get him into the *down*.
2. Say, "Down," when he lies down.

Repeat as often as you need to but not so much that he gets bored and tired. And never push him down; gently guide him by lowering your hand in front of him, using a treat if necessary.

The *down* command can be a lifesaver if your Maltese should escape from the yard or get loose from his leash.

THE *STAY* COMMAND

The *stay* command can be taught once your Maltese has learned to sit or lie down.

How to Teach *Stay*

1. With your dog on leash, tell him to sit.
2. Then face him, hold your hand out, palm toward him, and walk backward one step, saying, "Stay," in a firm voice.
3. If your dog stays where he is, praise him and give him a treat.
4. If he moves, simply ignore this behavior and start again, taking him back to his starting place and telling him to sit.

As he learns the command, you can increase the distance a little at a time. Repetition is the key to success, but keep training sessions short and fun so that your Maltese does not become bored. When you are finished with the *sit*, tell him he is a good boy and praise him, or perhaps give him a code word to let him know that the exercise is finished and he can get up.

THE *COME* COMMAND

The *come* command, also known as the *recall* in obedience training, could be another lifesaver if your Maltese ever gets loose. If he knows this command, you can call him back to your side, to safety, no matter what he is doing.

How to Teach *Come*

1. With your Maltese on leash, place him in a *sit–stay* and walk a few feet (0.5 m) away.
2. Face your dog and say, "Come," and wait for your dog to walk toward you.
3. Praise and reward him with a treat.
4. Repeat and gradually increase the distance between you.

Treats are not necessary, but since this is such a difficult command to learn, they may assist in training. Your Maltese should always associate the word "come" as a positive, not a negative. Don't show any anger or frustration, although sometimes you may feel that way. He should always *want* to come to you, not run away because he thinks he is going to be reprimanded.

If your Maltese is stubborn and will not come when you ask him to, calmly go to him, bring him back to where you started, and praise him. This teaches the dog that he must follow the command but shows that you are not angry about it.

THE *HEEL* COMMAND

A Maltese heeling nicely alongside his human is a beautiful sight to see, whether he has a long coat or an adorable puppy cut. Heeling is also one of the most useful behaviors a dog can have. It will help you navigate crowds and keep him from roaming into the path of others.

A Maltese heeling nicely alongside his human is a beautiful sight to see.

"Heeling" means your dog is walking beside you and not walking ahead of you, lagging behind you, or straying out to the side. The leash is there for security only; it is never used to drag your dog around or hold him in position. The idea is to condition him to want to be by your side rather than to force him to be there.

How to Teach *Heel*

1. Start by standing with your dog sitting very close to your left leg, both of you facing the same way. Have a treat in your left hand, up near your waist.
2. Say your dog's name to get his attention and to gain eye contact.
3. Take two steps forward and stop. If your dog moves with you, say, "Heel," and if he stops with you, enthusiastically praise him and give him a treat.
4. After he finishes his treat, repeat the process.
5. Once he is consistent, increase the distance. If your dog lags behind or seems inattentive, make a noise to get his attention and start over.

Once your Maltese becomes reliable with his heeling, up the ante and vary the exercise. Walk slowly, then faster. Try some left and right turns. Go to a different location. Ask someone to provide some distractions. Don't expect perfection unless you are heading for the obedience ring. The important thing is that he stay by you when on a walk, out of harm's way and as close to you as he can be.

FINDING A PROFESSIONAL TRAINER

Dog training is an unregulated industry. One way to identify a reliable trainer is to check with the Association of Professional Dog Trainers (APDT). Through annual conferences and networking, these trainers continue to improve their skills. Another factor to consider is whether the trainer participates in obedience, rally, or agility trials. If so, she has probably trained a number of dogs with different personalities and requirements.

The trainer you select should use methods that emphasize positive reinforcement. The Maltese thrives on attention and pleasing his human. There is no need for negative training techniques when positive methods are much more humane and so much fun to do. Good trainers are willing to openly discuss their methods and should give you an opportunity to watch a class without your dog before you enroll.

Consider whether the trainer has experience with toy breeds. Maltese are sturdy dogs, but they are not rugged dogs. They require gentler handling than our larger canine friends. If the class is crowded and your dog will be the only

Your professional trainer should use methods that emphasize positive reinforcement.

toy, consider finding a class with smaller dogs. This may not be necessary, as your author's small dogs have been in classes with large dogs for years without incident. It just depends on the nature of the other dogs and their humans. It is much better to attend classes where you will have distractions, constructive criticism, and plenty of socialization. Many of us have made lifelong (human) friends by attending these classes.

Check the dog clubs in your area—AKC kennel clubs, training clubs, etc.—to see if they offer puppy kindergarten or socialization classes. A pet store or private trainer may offer classes as well. Many people who sign up for one class enjoy the experience so much that they become involved in obedience trials and go on for AKC or UKC titles. Others branch into conformation showing as the "show bug" hits them.

Training your Maltese can be fun for both of you, whether you do it yourself, attend obedience classes, or use a private trainer. You will be amazed at your dog's potential to learn and the bond it will create between the two of you. The ultimate goal is a well-adjusted, happy family member.

SOLVING PROBLEMS
WITH YOUR MALTESE

Taking the time to solve problem behaviors will pay off with years of good manners.

The Maltese is one of the happiest, liveliest, brightest—and smallest—of all breeds. Because of his diminutive size and that ultimate cuteness factor, it is easy to look at him and see the perfect little pet. It is also easy to forget that he is a dog, with many of the same needs and requirements of the largest of his species.

One of these requirements is training. Many dogs are given up by their owners because of problem behaviors—and in most cases, something could have been done with the help of a trainer or behaviorist.

WHAT IS A PROBLEM BEHAVIOR?

Problem behaviors are canine behaviors that bother us when they happen. These are often natural behaviors that simply clash with your dog's environment, but they may also communicate more basic dilemmas (fear, medical problems, etc.) that we should help resolve. Dogs who show what we consider problem behaviors are messengers, not villains!

Generally speaking, Maltese are so eager to please, so quick to learn, that proper training techniques will eliminate most unwanted behaviors. However, Maltese are thought to be difficult to housetrain and a bit too zealous about alerting us with their barking. Other problem behaviors, which you can run into with any breed, are chewing, digging, jumping up, and nipping. Managing them may take extra work on your part, but the end result will be worth it.

The key to eliminating any of these behaviors is consistency. Follow through *every* time your dog misbehaves and encourage all household members to do so as well. Maltese have long life expectancies, so taking the time to train and modify your dog's behavior will pay off with years of enjoying a well-mannered pet.

BARKING

Barking, to a dog, is just normal canine communication. Dogs were probably bred to alert us from the beginning of our time together. We still want them to bark if someone is at the door or trespassing—or worse, if there is a fire. But to bark at every falling leaf? No.

Situations that may not frighten a larger dog may terrify a toy dog and trigger a vocal response. The key is to build the small dog's confidence and to reduce reactive barking. We can't yell at him when he barks; he'll just think we are answering back. If you punish him, it will just get worse. Persistent barking is not good for your dog either, as it could be causing him, and you, stress.

Think back to puppyhood. Did you unknowingly reward his barking? When the very young Maltese starts barking, we think it is charming, so he barks more. Then he does it to demand attention, and it is still somewhat cute. He learns eventually that all he has to do to get attention is bark. After all, this is his main form of communication, so how can it be so wrong?

WHAT CAN I DO?

If your Maltese is still very young, you can stop reacting to the barking in a positive way. Ignore him or tell him no. If the dog is older, you may have to take more drastic steps.

Sometimes dogs bark in order to alert you. Once you catch on to what he is trying to tell you, say, "Good dog," or "Thank you" for performing his duty when he first begins to bark. If this does not work, firmly say, "Enough," or "Use your inside voice," giving him a reward after he has stopped for five seconds or so. It may take quite a few attempts.

Some people have success using an empty soda can filled with a few coins or pebbles. When your dog starts barking, give him a command, such as "No bark," and shake the can. The noise should startle him and distract him from his barking. Once he has stopped barking, praise him and reward him with a treat.

Reward your dog when he is *not* barking in a situation where he normally does. If he is barking, try calling him to you and having him sit quietly, then rewarding him

with a treat. Be careful with this one. Don't let him train *you* to give him a treat when he barks!

Sometimes there is a reason for the barking. Your Maltese's favorite toy is stuck under the sofa. He is trying to get you to play or trying to tell you he has to go out. This type of barking is useful! Barking may also signal health issues such as deafness, dementia, or obsessive compulsive disorder (where repetitive barking is accompanied by pacing, spinning, and so on). Most importantly, monitor aggressive barking carefully to make sure the bite doesn't become worse than the bark!

CHEWING

The first thing newborn puppies do is use their mouths to nurse. As they get older, they use their mouths to—well, mouth everything. They use their mouths to carry things and investigate their surroundings. This behavior continues when they go to live with their new people. If this goes unchecked, it can become problematic as they chew on furniture, baby gates, our arms, and everything else they can reach.

WHAT CAN I DO?

Don't reprimand your Maltese after the fact. He won't make the connection. If you come home and find that he has chewed the stuffing out of your favorite pillow, greet him neutrally and put the pillow out of his reach. If he is standing there with his head and tail down, he is reacting to your tone of voice or body language, not feeling guilt. Just change the subject and let it go.

Consider that your puppy may be teething, especially at four months of age, and again at around seven months when the adult teeth start coming to the surface. Dampen a washcloth, twist it, and place it in the freezer for a few hours. Once it is nice and firm, offer it to the puppy to soothe his gums. Ice chips may also work. Massage his gums if he will let you. An older dog may start chewing if his gums hurt or if he has a loose tooth.

Regardless, strict supervision is going to be necessary. Dogs who are home alone a lot are the most likely to be chewers. Confine him away from any unauthorized chewables when you cannot watch him. A nontoxic bitter spray on the object of his chewing fascination may deter him from chewing. Test the surface first to prevent ruining your possessions even further!

There are a lot of different types of chew toys he can have, including rope toys (as long as they remain knotted) and indestructible rubber toys, which you can sometimes fill with treats to keep your dog occupied for quite a while. If your dog is confined in a crate with plenty of these toys, he should eventually redirect his chewing urge to the appropriate items. Rotate his toys every few days so that he doesn't become bored. (Don't put him in his crate as a punishment. That is his safe haven.)

The important thing to do is catch him in the act. If he begins to chew something, quickly say, "No" and substitute a toy he is allowed to chew. Encourage him to chew on the toy by playing with him and give lots of enthusiastic praise.

If your Maltese chews on *you*, cry, "Ouch!" Ignore him for a few seconds and then give him something he is allowed to chew. Praise him when he behaves. Surprisingly,

Dog Tale

When no longer useful to the Missouri puppy mill she lived in for ten years, Mira was auctioned off and found a wonderful home with Kay and Joe. Mira used to lie next to Kay during the night. She would often awaken from a sound sleep and sit bolt upright next to Kay as if she were trying to be sure she was really in a bed, not lying on wires as she had done for years. Once Mira saw that she was safe and "living her dream," she'd snuggle down close to Kay again and fall happily back to sleep. Often it just takes time to assure your dog he is safe and loved.

a lot of people think it is amusing for a puppy or even an adult dog to chew on their arm. This is not a positive form of communication for your dog!

And remember—there is no substitute for human interaction.

DIGGING

Dogs dig out of boredom or frustration. Or just for fun. Your dog may be attracted to your mulch, which could be dangerous if it contains cocoa or hazardous chemicals. He may see or smell another dog on the other side of the fence and want to join him, or more likely, her. With your Maltese's pristine white coat, you want to avoid this behavior at all costs, or you will face an immediate trip to the tub or the groomer.

WHAT CAN I DO?

If you know digging is a possibility, don't leave your Maltese where you can't observe him. If you do see him digging, interrupt the behavior right away with a loud noise or even your voice itself and then try to get him to concentrate on another activity. Since you are already in the yard, encourage him to run and play. Take a few of his washable toys out with him and try to burn off some of that excess energy.

If you don't mind that he digs, create a special digging place for him somewhere in the yard using nontoxic, sandy soil that's soft enough for those little paws. Bury a few treats in that section and then take him there, help him dig, and praise him when he complies.

HOUSE SOILING

What would cause a mature dog to suddenly start urinating in the house despite being given ample opportunity to do so outside? Has his routine changed? There are medical reasons and behavioral ones. Distinguishing between the two is important in order to determine the type and success of treatment.

MEDICAL CAUSES

Medical causes of house soiling include kidney disease, bladder infections, and diabetes. Epilepsy and spinal cord injuries can cause involuntary urination or defecation, and a virus or bacterial infection can cause loose stools or diarrhea. Incontinence is also common in older dogs. The geriatric dog who is showing signs of cognitive dysfunction, or "doggy Alzheimer's," may urinate in the home as his cognitive function and awareness of his surroundings decline.

A thorough medical history, including details about the volume, frequency, and color of the urine, can help point your vet in the right direction. Notice if your Maltese is straining or if he is leaking urine. Also be sure to note if he is drinking a lot of water. A healthy dog drinks up to one ounce (30 mL) of water per pound (0.5 kg) of weight daily.

PUPPY POINTER

Why is your puppy taking so long to housetrain? The rule of thumb for puppies is that they can "hold it" for a time span equal to one hour per month. So a three-month-old Maltese should be able to hold it for three hours. If your puppy is soiling his crate, he may not be getting enough opportunities to eliminate outside his crate.

Your vet may recommend drug therapy for elimination problems. This works by stabilizing the dog's mood and increasing his confidence, or in females, toning the bladder sphincter. Anxiety-reducing drugs may be effective when used simultaneously with training.

BEHAVIORAL CAUSES

Two common behavioral causes for house soiling are marking and submissive urination. These can be difficult to work with once the scent is present on your carpet or furniture, but they can be stopped with a little patience and consistency.

Marking

Normally, if you neuter a male Maltese at a young age, he will not have the opportunity to start marking his territory. Sometimes even older dogs will stop marking after being neutered, although it may take six months to a year for the hormones to subside. Marking indoors is often the result of territorial instincts.

When your male marks in the house, reprimand him (kindly!) during the behavior, not after. Clap your hands or say, "No," to interrupt him and then carry him outside. Praise him when he uses the correct spot (for example, a tree). The message is that urine marking isn't bad as long as it is outside. To be honest, this can be a hard habit to break. Belly bands can help catch the urine when your male attempts to mark and may deter him from marking.

Dominant females may mark, too, so don't be surprised to see your female lift her leg. Females produce small quantities of testosterone in addition to their own scent, which signals they are ready to mate. Spayed females usually cease this behavior, though occasionally they will urine mark when stressed or have accidents due to an age-related drop in estrogen levels. For females, panties or diapers can act as a deterrent.

Submissive Urination

This behavior is a little easier to work with but can be sad to witness. Submissive urination occurs when you greet your dog, bend over to pick him up, or scold him. He may also do this when he hears a loud noise. Dogs do not do this to be spiteful. The behavior goes back to the whelping box where puppies learn to be submissive to their mothers.

In order to correct this behavior, ignore your dog when you first get home—don't even look at him. After a few minutes, get down on his level—a long way for a Maltese!—and allow him to come to you. Reach out and scratch his chest. Talk calmly to him, and take him for his walk. Once he "does his business" in the appropriate spot, praise him. Be patient and try to build his confidence.

Help resolve submissive urination behaviors by building your dog's confidence.

WHAT ELSE CAN I DO?

Some dogs truly don't understand the rules or may worry about upsetting their mom or dad, so they will go find a spot in the house where they won't be seen. If you find this private indoor bathroom, just clean it up and forget it. Short of replacing all of your flooring, the only thing you can do is closely monitor your dog while you are home and confine him while you are not. Block access to favorite spots if you can. Try to totally eliminate the odor with an enzyme cleaner, or for example, by replacing a throw rug to deter your Maltese from eliminating there again. Simply masking the scent will not work.

It may be necessary to go back to crate training and make sure your Maltese knows the appropriate spots for his business. Make sure he is getting plenty of opportunities to go out. If you are not using a crate, confine him to one area of the house, or use baby gates or an exercise pen. Another option is to put him on a lead while he is in the house so that you will have control at all times. Once your little guy is housetrained, you can start giving him a little more freedom. Yes, we hate to see them in the crate. Yes, we want them on the bed with us. But a few months of solid training will be worth it for many years of happiness with your Maltese.

JUMPING UP

There is a huge amount of difference between a 5-pound (2-kg) Maltese and a 150-pound (68-kg) St. Bernard jumping up on people. The Maltese looks cute, especially if the jumping is followed by a perfect pirouette. The little guy is simply happy to see you after a long day, or anxious to meet your guest. Your guests might not think it is so endearing.

WHAT CAN I DO?

This is not a terribly difficult behavior to remedy. First, try acting disinterested when you arrive home and he starts jumping on you. Don't greet or pet him until he has stopped. If he is trained to sit and stay, that is even better. You can give him a *sit–stay* command, then say hello. If you bend down, he won't see the need to attempt to come up to your height.

Of course, you will have to ask visitors ahead of time to do the same thing. If you don't have a chance to do so, just pick up the little guy or put him in his crate until he has learned to stop jumping.

NIPPING

Puppies receive their first lessons from their dam, who growls when they grab too hard with their baby teeth while nursing. This is when a puppy starts to learn that behaviors have consequences. As he begins to play with his littermates, they will nip back if he tries it with them. This should be carried on by his humans, although we are not asking you to growl at or nip your puppy.

WHAT CAN I DO?

Gentle behavior should always be rewarded, but what do we do when the Maltese gets too rough? We can't fall into the trap of thinking, "Well, he is so small, what harm can he do?" You give him a nip and he will take a bite.

Your puppy may be trying to initiate play through nipping. If so, keep giving him toys to grab. A loud yelp or "No" may also be helpful. Never roughhouse or tease him with your hands, as that will encourage him to nip at your fingers. Be sure to monitor how other people, especially children, play with the dog.

Another method is to leave the room the second your dog gets too rough with his mouth. You don't have to leave him alone for very long. After a few minutes, come back and give it another try. Have him sit, and then reward him by playing with him gently. If he nips again, leave again. Have any children in the house participate in this exercise, too. This is too important not to be consistent about.

One popular method is called "nothing in life is free." First the dog learns the *sit* command. Then, whenever he wants something, he must sit before he gets it. He must sit for a treat. He must sit before you open the door for him. He isn't even allowed to jump on the sofa without sitting first. It isn't as harsh as it may sound, because dogs enjoy having a routine, but everyone in the household must participate for this program to work.

BE AWARE!

Many dogs are deathly afraid of thunderstorms. Reactions range from anxiety and trembling to soiling in the house and destroying furniture. There are several things you can try to help your Maltese during a thunderstorm. One is to provide a positive, distracting activity as soon as the storm starts. Treats, cuddles, and soothing music may help. Let your dog hide in his crate if he prefers—after all, it *is* his safe haven. During calm weather, you can desensitize him using thunderstorm CDs at low volume while plying him with treats and affection. Gradually increase the volume, getting to the loud booming sounds over a period of weeks.

If your dog nips or bites because he is afraid of being touched, rule out any medical causes for this behavior first. If it is a fear response rather than a medical cause, or if nipping progresses to full-fledged biting, you may need the help of a professional behaviorist.

WHEN TO SEEK PROFESSIONAL HELP

If your Maltese suddenly starts demonstrating perplexing behavior, have your vet evaluate him for possible medical causes. If it isn't medical, seek the services of a dog trainer or an animal behavior specialist. They are trained to see things in the dog's behavior that we often miss.

Before your visit with the trainer, keep a log of the who, what, when, where, and why associated with your dog displaying the problem behavior. Have family members help with the log so that you can determine if the dog behaves any differently with other family members. Write everything down—what may seem insignificant to you could be a major clue for the professional.

HOW TO FIND A BEHAVIORIST

People who work with animal problem behaviors are not regulated by any government agency, so they may have various titles and qualifications. One well-regarded type of behaviorist is the certified applied animal behaviorist (CAAB). The Animal Behavior Society (ABS) grants this certification to behaviorists who are academically trained, have experience in the field, and meet the ethical standards of the ABS.

Some CAABs are veterinarians who have completed a behavioral residency. These behaviorists can diagnose the medical cause of problem behaviors, often in coordination with your vet. If medication is required, they work with your vet in prescribing it and checking for any possible side effects along the way.

If you are fortunate enough to live near a veterinary school, most have behavior clinics or at least a behaviorist on staff. Some offer consultation phone lines where you can make an appointment with a behaviorist on staff to discuss the problem over the phone. There is usually a fee, and some request a video of the animal's behavior before the consultation. Although the fees are often steep, it is well worth the cost to be able to discuss the problem with a certified behaviorist.

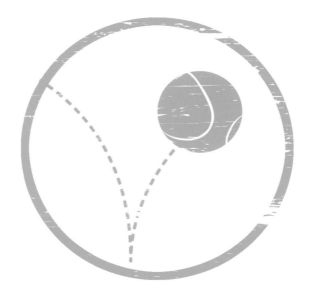

ACTIVITIES WITH YOUR MALTESE

There is nothing a Maltese wants more than to be with his human. There are so many things for you to do together, and findings have shown that spending time with your dog decreases your blood pressure, cholesterol, and triglyceride level. Dog sports and activities also provide a great way to meet and interact with other people. So this is a mutually beneficial partnership.

SPORTS AND ACTIVITIES

The number of events and titles offered by the American Kennel Club (AKC) has completely changed the world of dog sports. In addition to the traditional activities, there are now more casual events in which to participate. And keep in mind that if your Maltese is a rescue or even a Maltese-mix, or for any other reason does not have an AKC registration, he can still compete for titles!

AGILITY

You may have seen agility trials on Animal Planet or at a dog show. Agility is a fast-paced obstacle course that relies on nearly flawless communication between handler and dog. It is an amazing thing to watch. Because of the Maltese's high energy level and desire to please, it is not uncommon to see one at an agility trial. Many are champions in full show coat, going for that extra title, so it is truly a sight to see.

Agility courses feature obstacles such as tunnels, weave poles, and even tire jumps!

Passing the Canine
Good Citizen test can
open many doors for
your Maltese!

In an agility trial, the dog demonstrates his versatility by following cues from his handler through a timed obstacle course of jumps, tunnels, weave poles, and other objects. Teamwork is vital! This activity provides fun and exercise for both dog and handler, not to mention for the spectators!

In scoring, the handler and dog lose points if they go over the time set for the course or make mistakes such as taking an obstacle out of order, displacing a bar on a jump, or the handler touching the dog. A perfect score is 100 and the minimum is 85. And they don't grade on a curve! There are a number of titles to be earned in this fun sport, the highest of which is Master Agility Champion (MACH)—and there are MACH Maltese!

CANINE GOOD CITIZEN® PROGRAM

The Canine Good Citizen (CGC) program provides an indication that your dog has good manners at home and in the community. By passing ten basic steps, your dog can earn a certificate awarded by the American Kennel Club (AKC). You may be able to find a basic training class before you take the test, but you can also teach your dog the exercises yourself. Many kennel clubs, training clubs, and individuals offer the test, which must be administered by an AKC approved evaluator.

Before the test, you will be asked to sign the Responsible Dog Owner's Pledge. By signing the pledge, you agree to take care of your dog's health needs, safety, exercise, training, and quality of life. You also agree to show responsibility by cleaning up after your dog in public places, never letting him infringe on the rights of others, and so on.

Now your dog is ready for the test. These are the exercises he will be required to do, just to give you an idea. The AKC website will give you more detail.

1. Accepting a friendly stranger

2. Sitting politely for petting
3. Appearance and grooming
4. Out for a walk (walking on a loose lead)
5. Walking through a crowd
6. *Sit* and *down* on command and staying in place
7. Coming when called
8. Reaction to another dog
9. Reaction to a distraction
10. Supervised separation (from you)

All exercises are performed on leash. You may praise, encourage, and even pet the dog between exercises. Aggressive behaviors, such as growling and snapping, will result in disqualification. The AKC rewards dogs who pass the test with a certificate and placement in the Canine Good Citizen Archive.

BE AWARE!

Although the Maltese originated from a warm Mediterranean country, consider the weather before scheduling any outdoor activities where he may become overheated. The same applies to cold weather. If he must be in the cold, dress him in a coat or sweater and make sure his feet do not get too cold.

The Canine Good Citizen program is a great way to bond with your Maltese, and gives you an idea if the two of you would like to proceed to other activities. Passing the test will make your dog more likely to be accepted as a therapy or service dog. And further, some renters who normally will not rent to people with dogs may waive that stipulation if your Maltese has passed this test. There are many rewards for having a well-behaved Maltese!

CONFORMATION

Conformation showing remains the largest draw of dog shows, with more than three million entries annually. The dogs do not actually compete against each other. They are judged by how closely they meet the standard for the breed. The closer your dog is to the breed standard, the better chance he will have of doing well. Championship and grand championship titles are earned at conformation events.

In order to be eligible to compete, your Maltese must be at least six months old and AKC-registered (but not on a limited registration). Spayed or neutered dogs are not eligible to compete in conformation classes. Check out the AKC's website (akc.org) to see what shows are coming up in your area.

The AKC's New Exhibitor Mentoring Program gives you an opportunity to find out about conformation showing before you take the plunge. You can meet experienced dog handlers and breeders and learn about dog show etiquette, judging procedures, terminology, and so on. To apply for this program, visit the AKC website.

FREESTYLE DANCING

Believe it or not, you and your Maltese can show off your moves on the dance floor! Musical freestyle combines dog obedience and dance, with handlers and dogs performing dance-oriented footwork in time to music. This all began when a group of dog lovers joined to share an interest in creative obedience demonstrations and a love of music with inspiration from an equine sport called musical freestyle, a form of dressage. Although you normally see larger dogs in freestyle, toy dogs also participate.

Another well-known form is canine freestyle, a choreographed performance organized with music. Every movement is accomplished through the use of verbal cues and body language. The emphasis is always on the dog. The Canine Freestyle Federation offers titles in this sport.

OBEDIENCE

Obedience was first licensed by the American Kennel Club (AKC) in 1936 as a way to showcase canine intelligence and encourage deeper relationships between dogs and owners. The beauty of an obedience trial is that the dog and his handler (you) are judged on how closely the two of you match the judge's mental picture of a theoretically perfect performance. Maltese do very well in obedience. In the past ten years, entries have greatly increased at the American Maltese Association's national specialties, with a total of 30 entered at the 2014 event.

Obedience has three levels—Novice, Open, and Utility—which feature progressively more challenging exercises. Each time a dog receives a qualifying score in competition, he earns a "leg," and he must earn three legs for a title. Basic titles are Companion Dog (CD), Companion Dog Excellent (CDX), Utility Dog (UD), and Utility Dog Excellent (UDX). More advanced dogs and handlers can go on to earn other titles, such as Obedience Trial Championship (OTCH) and National Obedience Champion (NOC).

By the way—the person handling the dog is judged just as much as the dog is. Handler errors are penalized as much as any mistakes the dog makes.

RALLY

Rally was designed with the traditional pet owner in mind, but it can also be enjoyed at higher levels of competition. With the dog at the handler's left side, the team must navigate a course made up of designated stations, reaching signposts where they will be asked to perform tasks such as *sit, stay, down, come,* and *heel*. At advanced levels, at least one jump is added and the work is done off-leash. The judge watches for a smooth performance as well as skill in following the directions at each station. Scoring is not as strict as in traditional obedience.

Teamwork is a must. Handlers are allowed to clap their hands, pat their legs, or use verbal means of encouragement during competition (except when competing for the Rally Excellent and Rally Advanced Excellent titles, for which handlers are not allowed to clap their hands or pat their legs). Each performance is timed, but times are only counted if two dogs earn the same score. There are three levels—Novice, Advanced, and Excellent—and four titles—Rally Novice (RN), Rally Advanced (RA), Rally Excellent (RE), and Rally Advanced Excellent (RAE). As with other companion events, Maltese excel in rally because of their desire to please.

THERAPY DOGS

Therapy dogs provide comfort, a better quality of life, or educational experiences for people in hospitals, nursing homes, and various stressful situations. There is nothing like the unconditional love a dog can give. They counter feelings of loneliness with companionship. Through your participation in therapy dog activities, this boost can be shared by others.

A number of Maltese are certified as therapy dogs and do very well. Their size makes them portable and small enough to fit on laps or on the side of a bed. Having experienced the smiles and aura of calmness hospitalized people show upon seeing a 5-pound (2-kg) Maltese, stark white and sporting a bright red ribbon, your author can tell you this is a wonderful thing to do with your Maltese. You may find yourself there for longer than you anticipated, sharing your dog with people who need that pick-me-up in an otherwise dreary day!

Some areas provide for local therapy dog certification. Otherwise, you can work with national organizations, such as Therapy Dogs International (TDI) and Pet Partners (formerly known as The Delta Society), which provide

Dog Tale

We took Mouse, our Maltese, to an assisted living facility to visit our friend who needed a "dog fix." It took us forever to make it down the hall because people would see the dog and ask us to bring her into their rooms. We were virtually invisible, but Mouse was queen for a day!

numerous volunteering opportunities for qualified handlers and therapy dogs. You may also be able to find local programs for therapy dogs. Some libraries have their own "children reading to dogs" programs, and dog clubs often organize visitations to schools or nursing homes. Check with your local clubs to see what they have organized.

TRACKING

Tracking is the competitive form of canine search and rescue, where the dog demonstrates his ability to recognize and follow human scent. A human lays a track, leaving one or more items on the track with the final article at the end. The owner, who has not seen where the track goes, follows the dog on a long leash. She can encourage him but cannot give him any help. When the dog finds the item, the handler shows it to the judges. If the dog succeeds, he earns the tracking title for that level.

A dog can earn five American Kennel Club (AKC) tracking titles. The first four are Tracking Dog (TD), Tracking Dog Urban (TDU), Tracking Dog Excellent (TDX), and Variable Surface Tracking (VST). Champion Tracker (CT) is awarded to those dogs who have earned the TD (or TDU), TDX, and VST titles.

At least three Maltese have earned tracking or advanced tracking titles, including two tracking championships, as of this writing. Believe it or not, these small wonders can track with the big guys!

At least three Maltese have earned tracking or advanced tracking titles.

YOGA

While doing yoga may be easier with a larger dog, a Maltese is usually game for anything. Proponents claim yoga improves flexibility, reduces stress, increases positive energy, and resolves behavioral issues.

TRAVELING WITH YOUR MALTESE

Before making travel plans with your Maltese, consider how he might behave in unfamiliar surroundings. Will he be stressed? Will you have to leave him alone for long periods of time? Is there a chance he could escape? If he can be with you in his carrier or on a leash most of the time, chances are this outgoing, friendly little dog will enjoy the experience.

TRAVEL BY CAR

The safest way to travel with your Maltese by car is using a crate or airline bag. The goal is to keep him from jumping on you while you are driving or being thrown from the car in the case of an accident. And most importantly, never hold him on your lap while driving or as a passenger, especially if you are in a car protected by air bags. If your car has front-seat air bags, keep him secured in the back seat.

To be on the safe side, have information about your dog attached to the crate in case of an accident. Include his name, your name, your address, your phone numbers, your e-mail address, and any pertinent medical information about your dog. In a worst-case scenario, you should have a contact person to speak for the dog if you are unable to.

Special seat belts and harnesses work well with large dogs, but Maltese are simply too small for this type of restraint. Booster seats with adjustable tethers that also fasten to the seat belts may be an option for the back seat of the car.

If your Maltese has a tendency to become carsick, don't feed him the day you are traveling. If it will be a long trip, ask your vet about anti-nausea medication.

Always take along some water, but on longer trips, don't forget his food and treats (and some basic grooming tools if you will be gone for a few days). "Waterless canine shampoo" could come in handy for that errant mud puddle. Your dog's favorite toy will be much appreciated when he starts to get bored. Carry along some bags for poop pickup at rest stops.

Above all, never leave your dog in the car unattended. Even on cooler days, it takes only minutes for a pet to succumb to heatstroke and suffocation. In addition to temperature extremes, he could also hurt himself jumping or playing in the car. If there is no way around leaving your pet in the car, leave him at home.

TRAVEL BY AIR

The portability of your Maltese makes air travel so much safer because he is small enough to travel with you in the cabin in an approved airline carrier. Have his leash and collar handy for walking prior to departure, and make sure he has his identification tags on and is microchipped. Tape any essential information on his travel kennel, including his name, your home address, destination address, phone numbers, and e-mail address, and any medication he may need. Note that the owner of the dog is on board.

If your Maltese *does* have to fly in cargo, don't sedate him before the flight. Sedation can affect his respiratory and cardiovascular function, as well as his ability to maintain equilibrium. Most airlines won't accept a sedated animal at all. Airlines have policies against allowing live animals in cargo over and

PUPPY POINTER

Learning how to sit, stay, down, and come will make your Maltese puppy a better companion at home and away. Learning also stimulates his mind so that he doesn't become bored and restless.

Many hotels and motels now allow dogs, which makes traveling much easier.

under certain temperatures. If you have any doubts about the cabin pressure or temperature of the airplane, just don't risk it.

Airline regulations vary, so research the airline's pet policies before booking your flight. There may be limits as to how many dogs are allowed in the cabin at one time, so book early. A health certificate provided by your veterinarian within ten days will be required.

A health certificate and rabies vaccination are required for all travel abroad and for returning to the United States. The certificate is only good for ten days, so if you will be abroad longer than that, you will need to make an appointment with a vet there for a return certificate. Check with your vet, your airline, and the country to which you're heading for the complete range of required vaccinations. The United States Department of Agriculture (USDA) website at usda.gov is a good source for laws on international travel with your Maltese.

PET-FRIENDLY LODGING

More and more hotels and motels are allowing dogs, which makes traveling so much easier. Often there is a size limit, no problem for our toys, and a damage deposit, refundable or not. Ask up front what the policy is, and if no dogs are allowed, maybe they will make an exception for your well-mannered toy.

His crate will provide a familiar haven, as well as a safe place to keep him if you are out of the room when the housekeeping staff comes in. Take along plastic bags for cleanup and a bottle of carpet cleaner just in case. Avoid leaving him alone if he will bark. Barking indicates that he is stressed and not enjoying his vacation and it will disturb the other guests.

PET SITTERS

An alternative to taking your Maltese on vacation with you is hiring a pet sitter. There are professional pet sitters; there may also be a responsible teenager in the neighborhood. Some pet sitters stay at your house, while others come in several times a day to take care of your dog. Pets are happier and less stressed at home, and their exposure to illness is minimized.

RESOURCES

ASSOCIATIONS AND ORGANIZATIONS

BREED CLUBS

American Kennel Club (AKC)
8051 Arco Corporate Drive,
Suite 100
Raleigh, NC 27617-3390
Telephone: (919) 233-9767
Fax: (919) 233-3627
E-Mail: info@akc.org
www.akc.org

American Maltese Association (AMA)
www.americanmaltese.org

Canadian Kennel Club (CKC)
200 Ronson Drive, Suite 400
Etobicoke, Ontario M9W 5Z9
Telephone: (416) 675-5511
Fax: (416) 675-6506
E-Mail: information@ckc.ca
www.ckc.ca

Fédération Cynologique Internationale (FCI)
FCI Office
Place Albert 1er, 13
B – 6530 Thuin
Belgique
Telephone: +32 71 59.12.38
Fax: +32 71 59.22.29
www.fci.be

The Kennel Club
1-5 Clarges Street, Piccadilly,
London W1J 8AB
Telephone: 0844 463 3980
Fax: 020 7518 1028
www.thekennelclub.org.uk

Maltese Club
www.themalteseclub.co.uk

United Kennel Club (UKC)
100 E. Kilgore Road
Kalamazoo, MI 49002-5584
Telephone: (269) 343-9020
Fax: (269) 343-7037
www.ukcdogs.com

PET SITTERS

National Association of Professional Pet Sitters (NAPPS)
15000 Commerce Parkway, Suite C
Mt. Laurel, New Jersey 08054
Telephone: (856) 439-0324
Fax: (856) 439-0525
E-Mail: napps@petsitters.org
www.petsitters.org

Pet Sitters International
201 East King Street
King, NC 27021-9161
Telephone: (336) 983-9222
Fax: (336) 983-5266
E-Mail: info@petsit.com
www.petsit.com

RESCUE ORGANIZATIONS AND ANIMAL WELFARE GROUPS

American Humane Association
1400 16th Street NW, Suite 360
Washington, DC 20036
Telephone: (800) 227-4645
E-Mail: info@americanhumane.org
www.americanhumane.org

American Society for the Prevention of Cruelty to Animals (ASPCA)
424 E. 92nd Street
New York, NY 10128-6804
Telephone: (212) 876-7700
www.aspca.org

Royal Society for the Prevention of Cruelty to Animals (RSPCA)
RSPCA Advice Team
Wilberforce Way
Southwater
Horsham
West Sussex
RH13 9RS
United Kingdom
Telephone: 0300 1234 999
www.rspca.org.uk

SPORTS

International Agility Link (IAL)
85 Blackwall Road
Chuwar, Queensland
Australia 4306
Telephone: 61 (07) 3202 2361
Fax: 61 (07) 3281 6872
E-Mail: steve@agilityclick.com
www.agilityclick.com/-ial/

The North American Dog Agility Council (NADAC)
24605 Dodds Road
Bend, Oregon 97701
www.nadac.com

North American Flyball Association (NAFA)
1333 West Devon Avenue, #512
Chicago, IL 60660
Telephone: (800) 318-6312
Fax: (800) 318-6312
E-Mail: flyball@flyball.org
www.flyball.org

United States Dog Agility Association (USDAA)
P.O. Box 850955
Richardson, TX 75085
Telephone: (972) 487-2200
Fax: (972) 231-9700
www.usdaa.com

The World Canine Freestyle Organization, Inc.
P.O. Box 350122
Brooklyn, NY 11235
Telephone: (718) 332-8336
Fax: (718) 646-2686
E-Mail: WCFODOGS@aol.com
www.worldcaninefreestyle.org

THERAPY

Pet Partners
875 124th Ave, NE, Suite 101
Bellevue, WA 98005
Telephone: (425) 679-5500
Fax: (425) 679-5539
E-Mail: info@petpartners.org
www.petpartners.org

Therapy Dogs Inc.
P.O. Box 20227
Cheyenne, WY 82003
Telephone: (877) 843-7364
Fax: (307) 638-2079
E-Mail: therapydogsinc@
qwestoffice.net
www.therapydogs.com

Therapy Dogs International (TDI)
88 Bartley Road
Flanders, NJ 07836
Telephone: (973) 252-9800
Fax: (973) 252-7171
E-Mail: tdi@gti.net
www.tdi-dog.org

TRAINING

American College of Veterinary Behaviorists (ACVB)
College of Veterinary Medicine,
4474 TAMU
Texas A&M University
College Station, Texas 77843-4474
www.dacvb.org

American Kennel Club Canine Health Foundation, Inc. (CHF)
P. O. Box 900061
Raleigh, NC 27675
Telephone: (888) 682-9696
Fax: (919) 334-4011
www.akcchf.org

Association of Professional Dog Trainers (APDT)
104 South Calhoun Street
Greenville, SC 29601
Telephone: (800) PET-DOGS
Fax: (864) 331-0767
E-Mail: information@apdt.com
www.apdt.com

International Association of Animal Behavior Consultants (IAABC)
565 Callery Road
Cranberry Township, PA 16066
E-Mail: info@iaabc.org
www.iaabc.org

National Association of Dog Obedience Instructors (NADOI)
7910 Picador Drive
Houston, TX 77083-4918
Telephone: (972) 296-1196
E-Mail: info@nadoi.org
www.nadoi.org

VETERINARY AND HEALTH RESOURCES

The Academy of Veterinary Homeopathy (AVH)
P. O. Box 232282
Leucadia, CA 92023-2282
Telephone: (866) 652-1590
Fax: (866) 652-1590
www.theavh.org

American Academy of Veterinary Acupuncture (AAVA)
P.O. Box 1058
Glastonbury, CT 06033
Telephone: (860) 632-9911
www.aava.org

American Animal Hospital Association (AAHA)
12575 W. Bayaud Ave.
Lakewood, CO 80228
Telephone: (303) 986-2800
Fax: (303) 986-1700
E-Mail: info@aahanet.org
www.aahanet.org

American College of Veterinary Internal Medicine (ACVIM)
1997 Wadsworth Boulevard, Suite A
Lakewood, CO 80214-5293
Telephone: 303-231-9933
Telephone (US or Canada): (800) 245-9081
Fax: (303) 231-0880
E-Mail: ACVIM@ACVIM.org
www.acvim.org

American College of Veterinary Ophthalmologists (ACVO)
P.O. Box 1311
Meridian, ID 83860
Telephone: (208) 466-7624
Fax: (208) 466-7693
E-Mail: office13@acvo.com
www.acvo.org

American Heartworm Society (AHS)
P.O. Box 8266
Wilmington, DE 19803-8266
E-Mail: info@heartwormsociety.org
www.heartwormsociety.org

American Holistic Veterinary Medical Association (AHVMA)
P. O. Box 630
Abingdon, MD 21009-0630
Telephone: (410) 569-0795
Fax: (410) 569-2346
E-Mail: office@ahvma.org
www.ahvma.org

American Veterinary Medical Association (AVMA)
1931 North Meacham Road, Suite 100
Schaumburg, IL 60173-4360
Telephone: (800) 248-2862
Fax: (847) 925-1329
www.avma.org

ASPCA Animal Poison Control Center
Telephone: (888) 426-4435
www.aspca.org

British Veterinary Association (BVA)
7 Mansfield Street
London
W1G 9NQ
Telephone: 020 7636 6541
Fax: 020 7908 6349
E-Mail: bvahq@bva.co.uk
www.bva.co.uk

Canine Eye Registration Foundation (CERF)
P.O. Box 199
Rantoul, Il 61866-0199
Telephone: (217) 693-4800
Fax: (217) 693-4801
E-Mail: CERF@vmdb.org
www.vmdb.org

Orthopedic Foundation for Animals (OFA)
2300 E. Nifong Boulevard
Columbia, MO 65201-3806
Telephone: (573) 442-0418
Fax: (573) 875-5073
E-Mail: ofa@offa.org
www.offa.org

US Food and Drug Administration Center for Veterinary Medicine (CVM)
7519 Standish Place
HFV-12
Rockville, MD 20855
Telephone: (240) 276-9300
E-Mail: AskCVM@fda.hhs.gov
www.fda.gov/AnimalVeterinary/

PUBLICATIONS
BOOKS
Anderson, Teoti. *The Super Simple Guide to Housetraining.* Neptune City: TFH Publications, Inc., 2004.

Fernandez, Amy. *Maltese.* Neptune City: TFH Publications, Inc., 2007.

Morgan, Diane. *The Maltese.* Neptune City: TFH Publications, Inc., 2005.

MAGAZINES
AKC Family Dog
American Kennel Club
260 Madison Avenue
New York, NY 10016
Telephone: (800) 490-5675
E-Mail: familydog@akc.org
www.akc.org/pubs/familydog

AKC Gazette
American Kennel Club
260 Madison Avenue
New York, NY 10016
www.akc.org/pubs/gazette/digital_edition.cfm

WEBSITES
Nylabone
www.nylabone.com

TFH Publications, Inc.
www.tfh.com

BIBLIOGRAPHY

BOOKS
British Dogs: Their Varieties, History, Characteristics, Breeding, Management, and Exhibition. Hugh Dalziel, 1897.

The Complete Maltese. Nicholas Cutillo, 1986.

Dogs of China & Japan: In Nature and Art. V. W. F. Collier, 1921.

Dogs Through History. Maxwell Riddle, 1987.

Good Old Dog: Expert Advice for Keeping Your Aging Dog Happy, Healthy, and Comfortable. Nicholas Dodman, BVMS, 2010.

Lost History of the Canine Race: Our 15,000-Year Love Affair with Dogs. Mary Elizabeth Thurston, 1996.

The Maltese. Bobbie Linden, 1999.

The Maltese: Diminutive Aristocrat. Vicki Abbott, 2000.

The Maltese Dog: A History of the Breed. Dennis Carno and Virginia T. Leitch, 1970.

The Maltese Today. Vicki Herrieff, 1996.

The Power of Positive Dog Training. Pat Miller, 2001.

Toy Dogs and Their Ancestors: Including the History and Management of Toy Spaniels, Pekingese, Japanese and Pomeranians. The Honorable Mrs. Neville Lytton, 1911.

PERIODICALS
DogWatch
www.dogwatchnewsletter.com

Modern Dog
www.moderndogmagazine.com

National Geographic
"Wolf to Woof: The Evolution of Dogs." Karen E. Lange, January 2002.

Your Dog
vet.tufts.edu/publications/your_dog.html

WEBSITES

All Pets Dental Clinic
www.dentalvet.com/general.htm

American College of Veterinary Surgeons
www.acvs.org

American Heartworm Society
www.heartwormsociety.org

American Kennel Club
www.akc.org

American Maltese Association
www.americanmaltese.org

Association of American Feed Control Officials
www.aafco.org

Better Dog Care, Better Dog Nutrition (Sabine Contreras)
www.betterdogcare.com

Dog Food Advisor
www.dogfoodadvisor.com

The Dog Food Project
www.dogfoodproject.com

Dog Star Daily
www.dogstardaily.com

Explore Italian Culture
www.explore-italian-culture.com

Karen Pryor Clicker Training
www.clickertraining.com

Pet360
www.pet360.com

PetWave
www.petwave.com

US Food and Drug Administration
www.fda.gov

Veterinary Practice News
www.veterinarypracticenews.com

Vetinfo
www.vetinfo.com

WebMD
pets.webmd.com/dogs

WebVet
www.webvet.com

INDEX

A

accidents, housetraining, 100
activities
   agility trials, 122–123, **122**
   Canine Good Citizen
      program, 123–124, **123**
   conformation showing,
      124–125
   freestyle dancing, 125
   obedience trials, 125
   rally sport, 125–126
   therapy dogs, 126–127, **127**
   tracking competition, 127,
      128
   traveling, 128–132, **130**
   yoga, 128
acupuncture, 89
agility trials, 122–123, **122**
air travel, 129–130
Aldrovandi, Ulisse, 12
allergies, to dogs, 25
alternative therapies, 89–90
Alzheimer's type symptoms,
   114
American Kennel Club (AKC)
   breed standard, 16
   Canine Good Citizen
      program, 123
   Maltese first showing, 12–13
   microchip database, 37
   New Exhibitor Mentoring
      Program, 124–125
   obedience trials, 125
   tracking competition, 127
American Maltese Association
   (AMA), 13, 16, 125
American origins of Maltese,
   12–13

ancient Rome, origins of
   Maltese, 8–9, **8**
Animal Behavior Society (ABS),
   119
annual wellness visit, 73, **74**
Aristotle, 19, 21
Association of American Feed
   Control Officials (AAFCO),
   44–45, 49
Association of Professional
   Dog Trainers (APDT), 106
Athenaeus of Naucratis, 30, 42

B

baby gates, 30
balanced diet, 42–45
barking, 111–112
basic commands, 101–106,
   101–102, **104–105**
bathing, 60–62
beds, 30
behaviorists, 119
black points, defined, 18
body characteristics, 18–19
body condition score (BCS), 52
Bordetella (Kennel cough),
   76–77
boredom, 27
bowls, food and water, 34–35,
   34
breed standard, 16–21, **17**
breed-specific health issues,
   82–89
British Dogs (Dalziel), 16
brushing
   coat, 58–60, **59**
   teeth, 63–64, **63**

C

Caius, John, 10

calorie requirements, 42, **42**, 51
Canine Good Citizen program
   (CGC), 123–124, **123**
canned dog food, 46–47, **46**,
   49
car travel, 128–129
carbohydrates, in diet, 42–43
cats, companionability with, 23
certified applied animal
   behaviorist (CAAB), 119
characteristics
   coat and color, 19–20, **20**, **25**
   companionability, 22–25,
      22, **24**
   exercise requirements,
      26–27, **26**
   gait, 21
   general, 17, **17**, 18–19, 26
   head, 18
   hypoallergenic, 25
   legs and feet, 19
   living with your Maltese,
      21–22
   neck, 18
   physical, 16–17, **16**
   size, 20–21
   tail, 19
   temperament, 21
   trainability, 27
Charles V, Holy Roman
   Emperor, 10
Charlotte, Queen of England,
   10
chest characteristics, 19
chewing behavior, 112–114
Chico, Maltese dog, 11
children, companionability
   with, 23–25, **24**
chiropractic care, 89
choke chain collars, 32

clothing, 30–31, **31**
coat
    brushing, 58–60, **59**
    characteristics of, 19–20, **20**
    development of, 11–12
collapsed trachea, 82–89, **83**
collar tags, 37
collars, 31–33, **32**
color of coat, 19–20, **20**
combs, 35
Come command, 104–105
commercial dog foods, 45–47
companionability
    with cats, 23
    with children, 23–25, **24**
    with other dogs, 22–23, **22**
conformation showing, 124–125
congestive heart failure, 83
core vaccinations, 75–76
coronavirus, 77
crates, 33, 97–98
create training, 98
Cupid, Maltese dog, 10, 12

D
Dalziel, Hugh, 16
The Deipnosophists
  (Athenaeus), 30, 42
Delta Society, 126
dental care, 63–64, **63**, 83–84
diet. *See* feeding
digging behavior, 114
DogFoodAdvisor.com, 47
domesticated dogs,
    development of, 6–7, **7**
Down command, 103, **104**
dry dog food, 46–47, **46**, **49**
drying Maltese after bath,
    61–62

E
ear mites, 77–78, **78**
ears
    characteristics of, 18
    cleaning of, 64–65, **64**
    infections in, 64–65
Elizabeth I, Queen of England,
    10
English origins, 9
European origins, 9–10
exercise pens, 33–34
exercise requirements, 26–27,
    26
external parasites, 77–79
eyes
    characteristics of, 18
    cleaning around, 65–66
    health issues, 65, 67, 84–85

F
fashion accessories, 35, **36**
fats, in diet, 43, **44**
Federal Food, Drug, and
    Cosmetic Act, 45
feeding
    balanced diet, 42–45
    calorie requirements, 42,
      42, 51
    carbohydrates, 42–43
    commercial dog food,
      45–47
    dry vs. canned food, 46–47,
      46, **49**
    fats, 43, **44**
    foods to avoid, 51
    minerals, 44–45
    noncommercial foods,
      47–50
    obesity, 52
    proteins, 43–44

    quality of food, 53–54
    raw diet, 49
    schedule for, 50–51, **50**
    semi-moist foods, 47
    special diets, 47, **48**
    vegetarian diets, 49–50
    vitamins, 44
    water requirements, 45
    weight loss programs, 53
feet
    care of, 65
    characteristics of, 19
first aid, 90
fleas, 78
Food and Drug Administration
    (FDA), 46
food bowls, 34–35, **34**
freestyle dancing, 125

G
gait, 21
gay tail, defined, 19
general appearance and
    characteristics, 17, **17**, **25**, 26
Gibbs, Miss, 10–11
Giffard, Lady, 12
grain-free commercial dog
    food, 43
Greyhound combs, 35
grooming
    bathing, 60–62
    coat brushing, 58–60, **59**
    dental care, 63–64, **63**
    ear cleaning, 64–65, **64**
    eye care, 65–67
    as health check, 56–57
    nail care, 67–68, **67**
    professional groomers,
      68–69
    supplies, 35, 57–58

tearstains, 66–67, **66**
topknots, 62–63, **62**
grooming tables, **57**, 58

H
harnesses, 36
hazardous foods, 51
head characteristics, 18
health check, grooming as, 56–57
health issues
  acupuncture, 89
  alternative therapies, 89–90
  annual wellness visit, 73, **74**
  Bordetella (Kennel cough), 76–77
  breed-specific, 82–89
  chiropractic care, 89
  collapsed trachea, 82–89, **83**
  congestive heart failure, 83
  core vaccinations, 75–76
  coronavirus, 77
  dental issues, 63–64, **63**, 83–84
  doggy Alzheimer's, 114
  ear infections, 64–65
  ear mites, 77–78, **78**
  external parasites, 77–79
  eyes, 65, 67, 84–85
  first aid, 90
  fleas, 78
  heart murmurs, 85
  heartworm, 79–80
  hepatic microvascular dysplasia, 85
  herbal medicine, 89, **90**
  hookworms, 80
  house soiling, as symptom of, 114–115
  hypoglycemia, 45, 51

internal parasites, 79–81
leptospirosis, 77
Maltese encephalitis, 85–86
mitral valve dysplasia, 86–87, **86**
neutering, 81–82
noncore vaccinations, 76–77
obesity, 52
parasites, 77–81
patellar luxation, 87
periodontal disease, 63
portosystemic shunts, 87
reverse sneeze, 87–88, **88**
ringworm, 78
roundworms, 80
senior dogs, 90–91
spaying, 81
tapeworms, 80
ticks, 79, **79**
vaccinations, 73–77, **75**
vaccine titer, 74
veterinarians and, 72–73, **72**
whipworms, 80–81
white shaker dog syndrome, 88–89
heart murmurs, 85
heartworm, 79–80
Heel command, 105–106, **105**
hepatic microvascular dysplasia, 85
herbal medicine, 89, **90**
homemade diets, 47–50
hookworms, 80
house soiling, 114–117, **116**
housetraining
  crates and, 33
  technique, 99–101, **99**
  trainability and, 27
hypoallergenic dogs, 25
hypoglycemia, 45, 51

I
identification items, 36–37
indoor housetraining, 100
internal parasites, 79–81

J
jumping up, 117

K
Kennel Club, 12
Kennel cough (Bordetella), 76–77
kibble, 46–47, **46**, **49**

L
labels, dog food, 45–46
Ladies' Dogs As Companions (Stables), 21, 48
Ladies' Kennel Journal, 11
leashes, 31–33
leg characteristics, 19
leptospirosis, 77
licenses for dogs, 36
living with your Maltese, 21–22
lodging, pet-friendly, 130–131
Lytton, Mrs. Neville, 10

M
Maltese, names for
  lion dogs, 12
  shock dog, 11
    Ye Ancient Dogge of Malta, 8
Maltese Dog Club of America, 13
Maltese Dog Fanciers of America, 13
Maltese encephalitis, 85–86
Maltese Terrier Club of America, 13
marking behavior, 115–116

Mary, Queen of Scots, 10
microchips, 37
minerals, in diet, 44–45
mitral valve dysplasia, 86–87, **86**
modern era of the Maltese, 12
muzzle characteristics, 18

N

nail care, 67–68, **67**
National Dog Groomers Association of America (NDGAA), 68
National Maltese Club, 13
neck characteristics, 18
neutering, 81–82
New Exhibitor Mentoring Program, 124–125
nipping, 117–119
noncommercial foods, 47–50
noncore vaccinations, 76–77

O

obedience trials, 125
obesity, 52
origins of Maltese
   in America, 12–13
   American Maltese Association, 13
   in ancient Rome, 8–9, **8**
   coat development, 11–12
   domesticated dogs, development of, 6–7, **7**
   in Europe and England, 9–10
   history of, 8, **8–9**
   modern era, 12
   in royalty households, 10, **11**
   Victorian era, 10–11, **13**
other dogs, introduction to, 22–23, **22**

P

parasites, 77–81
patellar luxation, 87
pedicures, 67
periodontal disease, 63
   . See also dental care
pet carriers or bags, 37–38, **38**
Pet Partners, 126
pet sitters, 131
physical characteristics, **16**
Plutarch (Greek historian), 8
portosystemic shunts, 87
positive training methods, **94**, 95
problem solving
   barking, 111–112
   chewing, 112–114
   defining problem behavior, 110–111, **110**, **112**
   digging, 114
   house soiling, 114–117, **116**
   jumping up, 117
   nipping, 117–119
   professional help, 119
   . See also training
professionals
   behaviorists, 119
   groomers, 68–69
   trainers, 106–107, **107**
   veterinarians, 72–73, **72**
proteins, in diet, 43–44
Psyche, Maltese dog, 10–12
puppy kindergarten classes, 97
puppy tips
   bathing, 60
   housetraining, 115
   hypoglycemia, 45
   reputable breeders, 19
   training, 37, 100, 129

R

rally sport, 125–126
ramps, 38
raw diet, 49
rawhide chews, 39
recalls, dog food, 47
Responsible Dog Owner's Pledge, 123
reverse sneeze, 87–88, **88**
ringworm, 78
roundworms, 80
royalty households, 10, **11**

S

safety rescue stickers, 37
schedule, for feeding, 50–51, **50**
semi-moist foods, 47
senior dogs, 90–91, 114
shampoo, 35
shedding cleanup, 36
Sit command, **102**, 103
size characteristics, 20–21
skull characteristics, 18
Snips, Maltese dog, 13
snipy muzzle type, 18
socialization, 95–97, **96**
spaying, 81
special diets, 47, **48**
sport activities
   agility trials, 122–123, **122**
   conformation showing, 124–125
   freestyle dancing, 125
   obedience trials, 125
   rally sport, 125–126
   . See also activities
Stables, Gordon, 21, 48
Stay command, 104, **112**
steps, for dogs, 38

Stuart, Elizabeth, 10
submissive urination, 116, **116**
sunburn, **25**, 26
supplements, to diet, 44–45
    . See also feeding
supplies
    baby gates, 30
    beds, 30
    clothing, 30–31, **31**
    collar tags, 37
    collars, 31–33, **32**
    combs, 35
    crates, 33
    exercise pens, 33–34
    fashion accessories, 35, **36**
    food bowls, 34–35, **34**
    grooming, 35, 57–58
    harnesses, 36
    identification items, 36–37
    leashes, 31–33
    microchips, 37
    pet carriers or bag, 37–38,
        38
    ramps, 38
    shampoo, 35
    shedding cleanup, 36
    steps, 38
    toys, 38–39, **39**
    water bowls, 34–35

T
tail characteristics, 19
tapeworms, 80
tearstains, 66–67, **66**
teeth
    care of, 63–64, **63**, 83–84
    characteristics of, 18
temperament, 21
Thackery Rob Roy (Maltese), 13
The Dog: In Health and Disease

(Walsh), 11
therapy dogs, 126–127, **127**
Therapy Dogs International
    (TDI), 126
thunderstorms, 118
ticks, 79, **79**
topknots
    fashion accessories, 35
    grooming, 62–63, **62**
topline characteristics, 19
Topsy, Maltese dog, 13
Toy Dogs and Their Ancestors
    (Lytton), 10
toys, 38–39, **39**
trachea, collapsed, 82–89, **83**
tracking competition, 127, **128**
trainability, 27
training
    basic commands, 101–106,
        101–102, **104–105**
    create training, 97–98
    housetraining, 99–101, **99**
    importance of, 94–95
    positive methods, **94**, 95
    professional trainers, 106–
        107, **107**
    socialization, 95–97, **96**
    . See also problem solving
traveling, 128–132, **130**

V
vaccinations, 73–77, **75**
vaccine titer, 74
vegetarian diets, 49–50
veterinarians, 72–73, **72**
Victorian era, 10–11, **13**
vitamins, 44

W
Walsh, John Henry, 11

water bowls, 34–35
water requirements, 34–35, 45
weight loss programs, 53
wellness visit, 73, **74**
Westminster Kennel Club, 12
whipworms, 80–81
white shaker dog syndrome,
    88–89

Y
yoga, 128
Young, Mrs. C. S., 13

PHOTO CREDITS

DEDICATION

To Nicholas, Mouse, Tinkerbell, Venus, and the Inimitable Toby.

ACKNOWLEDGMENTS

I would like to thank Pamela Rightmyer, Joanie Carqueville, and Kay Prisella for taking time to share their love for and knowledge of the Maltese with me. Thanks to Vicki Fierheller, chair of the American Maltese Association Health Committee, for her medical expertise. Finally, thank you to the late Marjorie Lewis for giving us our first Maltese, Nicholas, my main man.

ABOUT THE AUTHOR

Jenny Drastura has been involved with showing and breeding dogs since 1984 and has been a member of the Dog Writers Association of America (DWAA) since 1988. She also belongs to the American Maltese Association (AMA) and the American Lhasa Apso Club (ALAC).

ABOUT ANIMAL PLANET™

Animal Planet™ is the only television network dedicated exclusively to the connection between humans and animals. The network brings people of all ages together by tapping into our fundamental fascination with animals through an array of fresh programming that includes humor, competition, drama, and spectacle from the animal kingdom.

ABOUT *DOGS 101*

The most comprehensive—and most endearing—dog encyclopedia on television, *DOGS 101* spotlights the adorable, the feisty and the unexpected. A wide-ranging rundown of everyone's favorite dog breeds—from the Dalmatian to Xoloitzcuintli —this series surveys a variety of breeds for their behavioral quirks, genetic history, most famous examples and wildest trivia. Learn which dogs are best for urban living and which would be the best fit for your family. Using a mix of animal experts, pop-culture footage and stylized dog photography, *DOGS 101* is an unprecedented look at man's best friend.

At Animal Planet,
we're committed to providing
quality products designed to
help your pets live long,
healthy, and happy lives.